Margaret,

Thank you for all of your hard work and enthusiasm. I read this book a while ago and thought it had some good insights. Since you're an entrep I figured it might be of additional enjoyment benefit. I enjoy working with you and all that you bring to our team.

Stacy

essons in

EXCELLENCE

from

CHARLIE
TROTTER

by Paul Clarke

TEN SPEED PRESS
Berkeley, California

Ten Speed Press
P.O. Box 7123
Berkeley, California 94707
www.tenspeed.com

Distributed in Australia by Simon and Schuster Australia, in Canada by Ten Speed Press Canada, in New Zealand by Southern Publishers Group, in South Africa by Real Books, and in the United Kingdom and Europe by Publishers Group UK.

Design by Toni Tajima
Cover photograph and photograph on page i by Paul Elledge

Library of Congress Cataloging-in-Publication Data on file with publisher.

ISBN-10: 0-89815-908-3
ISBN-13: 978-0-89815-908-0

Printed in China

8 9 10 11 12 — 12 11 10 09 08

CONTENTS

EXCELLENCE in Marketing, Publicity, and Sales

EXCELLENCE in Public Service

INDEX   258

ACKNOWLEDGMENTS

I would like to thank my team at Ten Speed Press, who helped to make my dream a reality. Diana Reiss brought her tremendous editorial talents to bear on the text, as did Jenny Morrison and Kathy Hashimoto. I'd like to especially thank Lorena Jones, who persuaded me to persevere when the going got tough and provided me with invaluable direction and indispensable insight. I'd also like to thank Aaron Wehner, who coordinated the project, and Toni Tajima, who created the striking design.

This book wouldn't exist if it weren't for Charlie Trotter, whose leadership skills, extraordinary vision, and passion for excellence inspired its writing. I thank him most for having the confidence in me to undertake the project. He spent nearly fifty hours answering my questions and providing me with information about his business, provided me with the names of customers and media who could offer further information, and freed up his staff to speak with me on many occasions. Not only that, dozens of days and nights he welcomed me into his restaurant to observe his operation and work alongside his team, taking notes, hanging coats, plating food, greeting customers, you name it. With Charlie Trotter and his business as models, my job was not only easy, but also eminently enjoyable and illuminating.

I owe my family a huge debt of gratitude. My parents, Dan and Bridget Clarke, and my sister, Stephanie, have provided me with unending support and encouragement over the years. I especially thank my lovely wife, Kathy, who not only has supported my efforts, but also has been a wonderful and patient mother to our two young children, Kevin and Jacqueline, while I have been moonlighting to complete this project for three years.

Yours truly,

Paul Clarke

INTRODUCTION by Geoffrey Smart

"What makes Charlie Trotter such a great chef?"

This question ran through my mind as the time came to be a chef-for-a-day in Charlie Trotter's kitchen. My family won the opportunity in a charity auction and knew I would love to spend a day in the world-famous kitchen. As an industrial psychologist, I help CEOs and venture capital investors assess people and improve companies. In the course of my career, I have advised self-made billionaires, Rhodes scholars, and brilliant scientists, but I have rarely seen a more impressive leader than Charlie Trotter. After nine hours in his kitchen, I observed that Chef Trotter (as his team calls him) demonstrates six core leadership skills that serve as lessons for those of us in the business world.

Hire the Best

Upon entering the kitchen at 2 p.m., I was immediately impressed by the quality of Trotter's chefs. Not an unshaven, untucked slacker was to be found in this group. Had they not been wearing the customary chef hats and jackets, I might have mistaken them for Goldman Sachs investment bankers. Chef Trotter scours the world for talent; the best stay, the rest go. Each of the twelve culinary artists had an air of professionalism, urgency, cheerful briskness, and confidence. A petite, poised woman greeted me at the door and whisked me off to convert my civilian clothes into chef's garb.

Teamwork

Charlie Trotter's kitchen is not a collection of individuals. It is a living, breathing beast with seventy-four legs and arms, all moving in a fast-paced ballet designed to produce the finest dining experience anywhere. It was interesting to note that everyone wore exactly the same outfit. There were no red jackets for sous chefs (Charlie's lieutenants) or a super tall hat for the Master Chef. At 4 p.m., the team all ate together. Throughout the evening, whenever somebody had a spare moment, he or she swept or mopped the floor to keep it spotless. Pitch in and help: work as a team.

Communication

Every person in the kitchen knows what everyone else is doing. Because the timing has to be perfect in order for a dish to come together and make it to the customer's table hot, communication is key. Also, because the kitchen is small, a failure to communicate might result in collisions, spills, or fires. In Trotter's kitchen, if you close your eyes, you can picture what people are doing because they announce everything: "Open!" when they open a cabinet door, "Coming through," or the more urgent "Coming through—hot!" when they really need to get by, sometimes followed by the more direct "Suck it in!"

Highest Standards

It should not surprise you that Trotter's buys the very best ingredients. But did you know that the restaurant's leaders actually visit farmers and suppliers and talk about ways to make the best even better?

At one point, after I had finished peeling some lemons, I watched a junior chef take five minutes to carefully arrange slices of duck on six plates. When he finished, the wait staff was not ready to deliver the minimasterpieces at precisely the right time. I heard the junior chef mutter, "Ah, it's not perfect now—not hot." Without hesitation, he disassembled each of the plates, replaced them with hot slices of duck, and said loudly, "I will have this for you in thirty seconds, please be ready." Charlie Trotter was not in proximity and did not have to tell anyone to replace the dish and make it perfect. That is the sign of a great leader—one whose high standards permeate the organization even when he or she is not there.

Innovation

Chef Trotter does not seem to be limited by convention in determining what ingredients go with what. He will be the judge of what tastes good together, thank you very much. Also, he encourages all of his chefs to suggest ideas and to experiment. This passion for innovation and willingness to listen to the good ideas from your people is how great leaders bend the paradigm and create a competitive advantage.

Truly Delight Customers

Everyone from Chef Trotter to the bussers appeared cognizant of the end goal of the restaurant: to truly delight customers. They delighted me when, after letting me bother them for a full workday, one of the sous chefs set up a small tablecloth and a glass of chardonnay. "Hungry?" he asked. "Sure!" I said, hoping to be offered a morsel of what we had just prepared. What followed was a nine-course meal suitable for a king, each course prepared and presented by a different chef.

So what was the man himself like? Charlie Trotter is a quietly intense man. He leads by example, gives very candid but constructive feedback, and is incredibly meticulous in a way that would make CPAs envious. When I was sprinkling some sage on a group of dishes, my blatant incompetence caught Chef Trotter's attention from thirty feet away. "You must sprinkle *around,* not just in the center," he said with the urgency of a neurosurgeon.

It is clear that his team has the highest respect for him as a person and professional. "We put our hearts into trying to meet his expectations," a young chef said. When asked whether they meet Chef Trotter's expectations, the young chef laughingly replied, "Almost!"

The day I spent in Charlie Trotter's kitchen I shall never forget. The cooking tips were plentiful, and the leadership lessons epic. Here's to you, Chef Trotter, for serving up your culinary wizardry and leadership lessons for us all.

Geoffrey H. Smart, Ph.D., is president of G.H. Smart and Co., Inc., a Chicago-based management consulting firm.

envisioning

EXCELLENCE

"When you have a true passion for excellence, and when you act on it, you will stand straighter. You will look people in the eye. You will see things happen. You will see heroes created, watch ideas unfold and take shape."

—TOM PETERS

"A true passion for excellence"—what does it mean in reference to Charlie Trotter's extraordinary vision and success? Many entrepreneurs have entered business using their wits and their imagination. Most have a taste for success, and scores have viable visions; these days more than a few of them are college graduates. If that's all Charlie Trotter had going for him, he'd be just another flash in the pan, stoked up with grand illusions.

But Charlie Trotter possesses what many other entrepreneurs lack: an unbridled passion for his work. "I run my kitchen the way Brando's Kurtz ran his outpost in *Apocalypse Now,*" Trotter told *U.S. News & World Report.* "Sometimes people think I'm operating without any restraint."

That "lack of restraint" may be just what makes Trotter extraordinary. As a chef, Trotter wasn't given formal training, nor did he learn his art in Europe. "I come from the American Midwest, from the heartland." And yet today, Trotter competes with the best of New York, the best of Europe, the finest chefs the world over. "From the start, I realized it's completely up to me how far I'm going to go. I could get comfortable on an easy level and coast. Or I can keep on striving and trying to do something that is exceptional: keep trying to assess my competitors in the field and figure out what is necessary to outperform them."

The chef lives and breathes fine food, wine, and dining. He unquestionably loves his profession and his business more than any other activity or interest. "If you strive like crazy for perfection," he explains, "at the very least you will hit a high level of excellence, and then you might be able to sleep at night." His fanaticism has paid off. Echoing praise offered by dozens of international food critics, *Rarities* magazine writes: "Trotter is a genius, producing meals that are truly culinary symphonies."

Passion is "emotion that is deeply stirring or ungovernable," according to the Webster's definition. It's a feeling and driving force that is almost beyond one's control. You, too, have passions—for music, fashion, literature, racecars, sailing, basketball, cooking, or some other aspect of human endeavor. Whether you're a manager of a restaurant or other service-industry business, CEO of a high-tech corporation, owner of a contracting company with a handful of employees, or budding entrepreneur dreaming up your business plan, the ultimate question is: do you have the required passion for your business or the one you intend to open? Passion is a key motivator, the element that separates average and good businesspeople from excellent ones.

To help you determine if you have what it takes, complete the following exercise. Circle the corresponding number (1 = complete disagreement, 3 = neutral, 5 = complete agreement) and see how you score. Above all, *be honest with yourself.*

When I get up in the morning, I can barely wait to get to work.
   1   2   3   4   5

I constantly think about my work and work-related issues.
   1   2   3   4   5

I enjoy reading industry-related journals more than any other materials.
   1   2   3   4   5

For fun, I frequently attend industry-related functions or events.
   1   2   3   4   5

Most of the books I read relate to my business or business in general.
   1   2   3   4   5

I never object to working twelve-hour days.
   1   2   3   4   5

I never regret missing social engagements because of work.
   1   2   3   4   5

My coworkers and former employers would describe me as very passionate about my line of work.
   1   2   3   4   5

When I speak to people about my work, they're excited to hear what I have to say.

   1   2   3   4   5

I am most happy when I'm working.

   1   2   3   4   5

I am most proud when I make customers happy.

   1   2   3   4   5

I am entirely committed to excellence.

   1   2   3   4   5

I truly believe in my work and my business.

   1   2   3   4   5

I demand that people who work for me love their work.

   1   2   3   4   5

When I receive recognition, I redouble my efforts and work harder than ever.

   1   2   3   4   5

I am most rewarded by work-related accomplishments.

   1   2   3   4   5

I am most disappointed by work-related failures.

   1   2   3   4   5

I am never completely satisfied with my or the company's achievements.

   1   2   3   4   5

I am very fulfilled by my work and my company's achievements.

   1   2   3   4   5

I am prepared to work as hard as I can in this profession until it's time to retire.

   1   2   3   4   5

If you score 91 to 100 on this exercise, you are very passionate about your work. A score of 81 to 90 indicates you need to *at least* consider new, different, or expanded responsibilities, while delegating a portion of your present responsibilities to someone else. A score of 80 or less means you ought to reexamine your career and business choice.

The fact is, you can't make yourself passionate. Many restaurateurs, for example, open establishments for the wrong reasons. They see glamour, money, publicity, even celebrity, but they fail to see stiff competition, never-ending hard work, and huge responsibilities. A staggering 90 percent of new restaurants fail within five years, according to the National Restaurant Association, and often it's because they were opened by restaurateurs who are not committed to excellence and who do not love their work. If you determine you're not really passionate about what you're doing, figure out what really floats your boat.

Trotter believes analysts can accurately predict which businesses will fail and succeed based on their leaders' passion for the work and the business. "Too often people do work they're not really in love with," says Trotter. "They have an idea they've cooked up, some moneymaking scheme, for example, and they're talented at producing it or marketing it. But they're not totally driven by a passion. That's going to be the difference between whether they succeed or not. People who are passionate will find a way to make their businesses excellent despite all else."

As part of their studies, Northwestern University and University of Chicago business school students are often asked to develop plans for hypothetical businesses that they believe would succeed. These budding entrepreneurs frequently call Chef Trotter, asking him to describe how to create a successful restaurant—though they lack any background in cooking or customer service, nor claim any great love for the restaurant business. Says Trotter, "To me this is not how business works. Such course exercises are virtually useless. You don't come up with the best theoretical plan and then just do it," explains Trotter. "Students shouldn't be taught merely to chase business or marketing opportunities. We should be producing entrepreneurs who are passionate about their own business and are eager to devise a way to make it excellent. The goal has got to be from the heart; you've got to really believe in what you're doing. And then carrying it out becomes automatic, like breathing. Nearly effortless."

Examine Your Values
Rather Than Everyone Else's

Any contemporary business guide will say that a company must have a dynamic vision in order to survive. These books describe the corporate blueprints of Fortune 500 companies from Hewlett-Packard to Microsoft to McDonald's. Presumably, the reader can choose a proven model, ape it, and come out wildly successful. The problem? Visions need to come from within, not from the inspiration of some other company's annual report.

A truly powerful company vision is founded on your most cherished principles, values, and standards. There's no way to fake it. Present a false vision, and your employees, customers, and competitors will see through it. For decades, Sears Roebuck and its department stores flourished. The company's values were reflected in its promise— "quality at a decent price." In the 1980s, with yuppie tastes for hot foreign cars, gourmet kitchen items, and name-brand clothing on the rise, Sears decided to join the pack—or at least try to fake the look. They failed, and stores shut down across the country.

When Charlie Trotter first conceived of his now-celebrated restaurant, he set out to create a culinary masterpiece. He knew his own personal vision would be its heartbeat. It had to be precise and it had to be true. To define his vision, Trotter didn't study the guiding concepts of other companies. Instead, he examined his own values.

The principles that excite and drive him, he found, were dedication, determination, integrity, attention to detail, consistency, and generosity. Using these as guidelines, Trotter drafted a company vision that is authentic, inspirational, and exacting: Charlie Trotter's restaurant would do whatever it took to consistently provide excellence in wines and cuisine, atmosphere, and service.

What values make *you* tick? You probably see integrity, sincerity, honesty, commitment, perseverance, consistency, attention to detail, determination, responsibility, generosity, and charity as imperative, indispensable values. The important question is, which principles will you put into practice on a *daily* basis?

Before you begin this exercise in self-examination, get ready to grapple with some real questions. Look at each value in detail, exploring as many facets of it as possible. You probably won't measure up on every single value, standard, or quality, but no one expects you to be a saint. It is important, however, to answer these questions *in writing* with complete honesty. Seeing the answers in black and white will give you a clear idea of which values you truly practice and help you formulate a reasonable and meaningful vision for the future.

Let's start with integrity and sincerity. Do you ever look for shortcuts or compromise quality in any endeavor? Do you believe it's necessary to purchase high-quality supplies and raw materials? Is your work always of superior quality? When you recognize your work is deficient, do you always tell your clients or customers? Are you ever guilty of saying one thing and doing another?

Say your firm is offered a major consulting assignment or project, but you suspect you haven't enough employees available to handle the work. Does honesty guide your chosen course of action? Perhaps you seek to hire someone to do bookkeeping, but the position involves a fair amount of administrative work, too. Do you make crystal clear the number of hours that person will spend answering phones, typing envelopes, and filing invoices? How do you feel about padding your expenses or overbilling your clients or customers?

Now let's look at commitment and perseverance. Though it might not be necessary, are you *willing* to work five or six twelve- to sixteen-hour days a week in order to create and maintain your business? Trotter never works less than a eighty-hour week, for example. Do you feel personally obligated to make your business an excellent enterprise? Do you sometimes take it easy on the job? How do you handle setbacks?

With respect to consistency, do you believe it's important to set very specific standards for certain job functions? Is your work or your company as good as it can be every day? Do you and your employees work hard every single day? What does diligence mean to you? Do you feel energetic every single day? Do you approach your work each day with the same earnestness and enthusiasm?

Any business owner needs to be fairly detail-oriented. Do you like to keep your office or your company clean and well organized?

Do you become furious when a document or letter was mailed without being proofread first? Do you hate to see someone with a crooked tie and unlaced shoe?

True determination and dedication are relatively rare qualities. Are you single-minded of purpose? Do you sacrifice leisure activities to see that your business improves? Would you do practically anything to make your business excellent? When everyone tells you you're nuts and your vision will never work, what is your reaction?

Do you believe responsibility is critical to excellence? When employees are late, don't show up, or shirk responsibilities, how do you react? When someone promises to deliver something or complete a project and drops the ball, how do you respond?

TO DEFINE HIS VISION, TROT-
TER DIDN'T STUDY THE GUID-
ING CONCEPTS OF OTHER
COMPANIES. INSTEAD, HE EX-
AMINED HIS OWN VALUES.

Generosity is another important value. When it's time to review employees, do you prefer to give everyone a cost-of-living increase or do you prefer to reward good work handsomely? Do you offer benefits, which are perhaps above and beyond the call of duty, such as leaves of absence, 401(k) plans, profit sharing, or flexible hours?

Finally, what is your idea of charity? Do you give a fair percentage of your disposable income to worthy organizations? Do you volunteer or host benefits for community groups or fund-raising organizations?

As a result of this exercise, you should better understand which values govern your work and relationships and which ones play a less important role. Once your view of yourself and your own values assessment is complete, it's time to do something even more courageous: get second, third, and fourth opinions. Copy the following list and make any additions you require. Choose three or more people who know you well—your spouse, siblings, parents, colleagues, friends, or employees—and request that they rate your adherence to these values. Tell them you've asked a number of people to answer the questionnaire with complete honesty, and give each a stamped, self-addressed envelope to send you the results anonymously. Afterward, compare your self-assessment with the answers your friends and associates provide.

VALUES ADHERENCE TEST

1 = never practices this principle   5 = always practices this principle

Integrity	1	2	3	4	5
Sincerity	1	2	3	4	5
Honesty	1	2	3	4	5
Commitment	1	2	3	4	5
Perseverance	1	2	3	4	5
Consistency	1	2	3	4	5
Attention to detail	1	2	3	4	5
Determination	1	2	3	4	5
Dedication	1	2	3	4	5
Responsibility	1	2	3	4	5
Generosity	1	2	3	4	5
Charity	1	2	3	4	5

If you score 1s and 2s on most of these values, put down this book and seek professional help.

All kidding aside, notice whether the answers your friends and associates provide match your self-assessment. From these results, you will be able to determine the four or five values or principles that resonate with your own, those that govern your work and relationships and those that play a less important role. Perhaps you'll discover that you value honesty, charity, and perseverance more than anything else. Perhaps dedication, generosity, and integrity are at the top of your list. In any case, when you create a vision for your business, you want to consider these values.

3 Do What Fulfills You

Many people find that if they aren't doing what they do best, they are miserable. Charlie Trotter is a case in point. The man needs to be running a superb restaurant, authoring books, consulting for outside companies, and participating in public service organizations. "I need to do something significant, to be able to affect my clients and the people who work for me and to give something back to the neighborhood, the community, and the city." Doing so invigorates Trotter and makes him feel like he's living up to his potential.

Clinical psychiatrists like Dr. Howard Alt have witnessed this phenomenon and know it well. In Charlie Trotter's case, Alt knows it intimately, since the psychiatrist also moonlights from time to time in Trotter's kitchen. "Charlie has to do this to be alive," Alt observes. "He would go under psychologically if he wasn't. He has to be doing his thing, and so do the rest of us. If we aren't doing our thing, we're dead in the water." When it comes to work, few things are worse than believing your capabilities, talents, skills, and experience are being overlooked or wasted.

As the boss of your own life, you can take action to make sure your unique resources and interests are utilized to the greatest effect.

Publishing industry CEOs are famous for taking advantage of this option. In addition to the universal responsibilities of entrepreneurship that their position entails, publishers also participate in various industry-specific functions, including writing, merchandising, publicity, and business development. One executive might spend more time on marketing, another on acquisitions. Still others—such as Mortimer Zuckerman of *U.S. News & World Report,* who writes regular editorial columns—make time for the work that truly moves them.

While creating new challenges can be that great kick in the pants that gets you going, you need to satisfy several other psychological needs to keep yourself engaged and zealous. For most successful leaders, a key component for self-actualization is satisfying the need to make a genuine contribution to the organization, industry, and community. In addition to achieving excellence and finding deep fulfillment, many also need to be striving for something higher.

Charlie Trotter cites a newspaper article he came across several years ago, which he clipped and mounted in his office. The piece profiled a young African-American student from Chicago's hard-edged West Side. The young man's parents had been absent from his life since childhood, and he'd grown up instead with his maternal grandmother. Drugs and crime ravaged his neighborhood, yet not only had the young man achieved high school honor student status, he also became a star basketball player with offers of full scholarships to several prestigious universities. The high school senior gave a simple explanation for his determination and drive: the year he turned thirteen, his grandmother had given him a picture with a cross-stitched message that read, "God's gift to you is your life. Your gift to him is what you do with your life." According to the young man, reading that message daily helped him to strive for self-fulfillment. Comments Trotter, "The message is extremely important. You owe it not only to yourself but to God to make something of yourself, to realize your full potential as a human being." No matter where you fall on the spiritual or religious spectrum, to foster that passionate inner drive needed to excel in your chosen field, you need to do what fulfills you.

At his restaurant, Charlie Trotter understands this concept well, eventually placing each of his veteran chefs where their greatest talents and interest lie. Some chefs are essentially administrators, spending most of their time ordering products and equipment and hiring, training, and scheduling employees. Others are on the front lines every day, developing dishes, cooking, and managing the rest of the kitchen. Still other chefs are involved in one or more of the many components of Trotter's: they write cookbooks, perform public relations, create retail products, consult to major corporations, and appear on his TV show. To deliver excellence, Trotter knows that staff members must work at jobs that reflect their essence, the areas that they will find most fulfilling.

It's time to answer some self-searching questions that will help you discover which management and entrepreneurial activities allow you to fully realize your potential and which ones only partly fulfill you. Take out a piece of paper so you can write out your answers, and let's get to work:

Teaching employees is the responsibility of every small business, but it might or might not be something that fulfills you. Ask yourself: How do I feel when I'm teaching? How would I characterize my confidence and comfort level? How are my communication skills? Am I articulate? How well do I know the material? How well do my employees understand the subject when I teach? How do they respond to the material? Do they respect me as a teacher? Are my employees attentive and engaged? Do I enjoy teaching? Does teaching make me feel good about myself?

Training is another management activity. Ask yourself: How are my skills as a trainer? Am I able to perform several jobs in the company? How well do I know the actual work employees do on a daily basis? Do I have sufficient patience and tolerance? On the other hand, am I tough enough to be a good trainer? Are employees who train under me well trained? Are my managers better at training than I am? Is training fun or a hassle? Do I have enough time to be involved in training? Does training make me feel like I'm making a difference?

Researching will more than likely be a necessary part of running a business. Ask yourself: Do I have strong knowledge of technical support resources? When there is a problem, am I able to solve it easily? When I need information, where do I turn first? Am I able to locate information quickly and easily? When experiments fail, how do I react? Am I persevering? Do I enjoy the research process? Is research rewarding?

What about **selling**? Ask yourself: Have I attended sales seminars or had formal training? How are my listening skills? In general, do I make people feel comfortable? How strong is my distribution and sales network? Do I understand the needs of my customers? Do I have sufficient knowledge of our company's products or services? Am I willing to stick with it as long as it takes to make the sale? How do I handle rejection? How well do I convey what our company offers? Does selling make me feel good and fulfilled?

Marketing may be your passion, or it may leave you cold. Ask

"CHARLIE HAS TO DO THIS TO BE ALIVE. HE WOULD GO UNDER PSYCHOLOGICALLY IF HE WASN'T. HE HAS TO BE DOING HIS THING, AND SO DO THE REST OF US. IF WE AREN'T DOING OUR THING, WE'RE DEAD IN THE WATER."

— Dr. Howard Alt, clinical psychiatrist and part-time chef at Charlie Trotter's yourself: Do I know the components of a good advertising message? Have I designed a market research study? Do I find research interesting? How would I rate my skill as a market researcher, creative writer, or artist? Do I understand media buying? With respect to public relations, how well do I understand the needs of media? Am I comfortable promoting myself? Do I enjoy analyzing demographics and statistical data? Do I enjoy the marketing process? Do I have a knack for marketing? Does marketing work make me feel like I'm making a contribution?

While **innovating** is the entire staff's responsibility, many entrepreneurs spend a good deal of time attempting to discover new or improved ideas, methods, or devices. Ask yourself: How strong is my knowledge of work processes and methods? Am I fond of analyzing opportunities? Do I know what needs to be improved? How do I react when customers tell me things need to be improved? How do I usually proceed when I have an innovative idea? Am I overly cautious or reckless? Does innovation get my motor running? When I innovate, do I feel like I'm doing some good?

Supervising is key to maintaining excellence, but that doesn't necessarily mean you have to watch over your employees' every move. Ask yourself: Am I able to be sufficiently firm with employees? Am I too hard on employees? Do I enjoy observing my employees at work? Do my managers know my values well enough to be the primary supervisors? Does supervising fulfill me?

Ask yourself: Though I have many other responsibilities, does performing our core work make me happiest? Does it leave me with the sense that I am following my true destiny? Is my time best spent doing the work of the company? Is this the work that makes me feel fulfilled? Is this work the reason I started this business in the first place? Am I fulfilled by teaching others how to do the work as well as I do? Could I delegate the work and be more useful and fulfilled building the business, selling, or marketing?

Don't just draw within the lines. Beyond your core work, there may be industry-related pursuits that better allow you to realize your potential. Charlie Trotter takes great pleasure in speaking to industry peers and business school students, writing cookbooks, and consulting to major food service companies. Ask yourself: With which other pursuits do I have the capacity to be involved? Are there committees on which I could serve? Are there businesses that could use my consultation? Which industry-related activities do I enjoy? Do they allow me to reach a larger audience with my message? Can I contribute more by doing these things? Do these activities help me to realize my potential?

After you answer these questions, reflect on all these activities. Using the following list, rate your ability with respect to each function on a scale of 1 (a major weakness) to 5 (a major strength). Then rate your level of satisfaction on a scale of 1 (not at all satisfying) to 5 (highly satisfying). Add to the list work-related functions and industry-specific pursuits.

	1 = major weakness 5 = major strength					1 = not at all satisfying 5 = highly satisfying				
Teaching	1	2	3	4	5	1	2	3	4	5
Training	1	2	3	4	5	1	2	3	4	5
Researching	1	2	3	4	5	1	2	3	4	5
Selling	1	2	3	4	5	1	2	3	4	5
Marketing	1	2	3	4	5	1	2	3	4	5
Innovating	1	2	3	4	5	1	2	3	4	5
Supervising	1	2	3	4	5	1	2	3	4	5

WORK-RELATED FUNCTIONS

_____	1	2	3	4	5	1	2	3	4	5
_____	1	2	3	4	5	1	2	3	4	5

INDUSTRY-SPECIFIC PURSUITS

_____	1	2	3	4	5	1	2	3	4	5
_____	1	2	3	4	5	1	2	3	4	5

Conclusions: You already realize that just because you excel at something doesn't mean it's necessarily satisfying or fulfilling, either practically, physically, esthetically, or spiritually. Many good salespeople, for instance, don't enjoy selling. As a rule of thumb, weigh fulfillment more heavily than capability. Activities that are highly satisfying *and* major strengths ought to be the functions you perform most frequently.

4 Know What the Hell You Want Your Company to Be

and Tell Everyone

"Know what the hell you want to be," says *Chicago Tribune* restaurant reviewer Phil Vettel. "It's a lot easier for customers to know what you are when *you* know. And Charlie Trotter does that better than most."

Vettel's advice and Trotter's practice are backed up by the most respected business experts in the country, including management guru Tom Peters, whose classic text, *In Search of Excellence: Lessons from America's Best Run Companies* (New York: Warner, 1988), surveyed the workings of dozens of extraordinary U.S. firms throughout the 1980s and '90s. Wrote Peters in his findings, "Every excellent company we studied is clear on what it stands for, and takes the process of value shaping seriously. In fact, we wonder whether it is possible to be an excellent company without clarity on values and without having the right sorts of values." Organizations that performed more poorly, he found, were characterized by one of two different features. Many, according to Peters, had "no set of coherent beliefs." The rest of these weaker companies may have had clear and well-known objectives but were excited and stimulated only by quantifiable goals: financial milestones, such as earnings per share or growth measures.

For Charlie Trotter, single-minded obsession with financial achievement was never a real threat. From the first, Trotter's business objectives went beyond the quantitative. When he decided to open his restaurant, he recognized there was an opportunity, particularly in Chicago, to open an establishment that was hands-down superior. Plenty of restaurants were beautifully designed and appointed. Some had award-winning wine lists. More than a few had excellent food. And here and there, a rare operation offered truly remarkable service.

But Trotter saw that no restaurant in Chicago and very few in the world could boast of every one of these stellar attributes. He therefore set out to create one. The young chef knew he had the wherewithal to pull it off: he was creative, had considerable industry experience, remarkable physical stamina, and excellent motivational skills. Trotter could also recognize superior quality when he saw it, and knew he could motivate employees to strive for excellence. So he developed a vision that was bold but (in his own mind at least) eminently "do-able."

Knowing What You Want Your Company to Be

At this point, you know which values are most important to you. They will become the foundation on which you build your business, governing your decision-making and leadership styles, employee training, management, and marketing. Now it's time for you to consider—or reconsider—what you want your company to be.

First, take a look at the competition. Like Trotter, you're aiming to find an unfilled industry niche. Sure, you've got to count on your own indisputable brilliance—but you also better back it up with research. To research marketing strategies of a competitor, one might read trade journals, visit a sales outlet, or try out the service that the competitor offers. Calling a company's customer service line can also be quite revealing. Obviously, your research methodology will depend on the industry involved. In the restaurant business, research involves eating out and reading the food section of your city's newspaper and magazines. A novel venture such as an ecological dry-cleaning business would require analysis of the chemical cleaning agents and efficacy of the alternative cleaning methods along with a study of profit projections based on an environmentally concerned target group.

Indeed, whether you plan to open a gourmet food emporium, a health spa, or a printing shop, take some time to analyze who's doing what in your area and region of the country. As an entrepreneur planning to open an upscale boutique, fine restaurant, or cutting-edge fitness club, for instance, there's no point in looking at discount clothing stores, fast-food chains, or cut-rate gyms. If you're going to be the best, nothing but the exceptional can serve as your model.

Begin a reporter's notebook, and investigate what's out there. Write down your findings so you can refer to them later. Consider the following questions, and take note of every impression. What seems an insignificant detail now could prove invaluable when your business is in full swing.

Describe the **customer service** of the typical rival. Is it friendly and courteous? Is it knowledgeable and helpful? How could it be improved? Is it fast and efficient? Do they offer delivery? Product guarantees or warranties? Hassle-free returns? Convenient hours?

What about **technology**? Are competitors equipped with modern technology, such as scanners, touch-screen computer monitors, word-processing systems, or frequent customer identification systems? Are local competitors on the World Wide Web? Do they have sophisticated security systems?

Marketing is another function you will want to investigate. Do competitors advertise? How well-conceived are their campaigns? How could they be improved? In what media do they advertise? Do they offer frequent sales promotions? Do they publicize themselves? Do they distribute catalogs or direct mail? What is the quality of these mailers? How could they be improved? Do most offer premium or value pricing? Do they offer everyday low prices?

If they are retailers, consider their **merchandising** and store **design**. What kinds of fixtures and shelving systems do they use? Is there a lot of clutter? Do they feature products well? How could their product displays be improved? Are store designs conventional or sleek and contemporary? Is the lighting soft or dramatic?

Now think about **product quality** and **product selection**. How would you describe the competition's product quality? Are the inputs or raw materials the best they can be? How could you find better? Is the manufacturing process of high quality? How could you do better? Do they offer a wide variety or narrow selection of products? Is the product selection diverse, eclectic, or straightforward?

Innovation is another area you might be able to exploit. Do competitors innovate regularly? Do they bring innovations to market quickly? Are their innovations truly new ideas or merely "me-too" items?

With the answers to these questions in hand, you'll end up with a fair idea of what's currently offered by the competition. You'll also know your rivals' strengths and weaknesses. The next step is to determine your own plusses and minuses. Again, get out a piece of paper and pencil. This time, rate yourself on the following characteristics:

	1 = poor			5 = superior	
Creativity	1	2	3	4	5
Artistic ability	1	2	3	4	5
Communication skills	1	2	3	4	5
People skills	1	2	3	4	5
Management skills	1	2	3	4	5
Motivational skills	1	2	3	4	5
Organization skills	1	2	3	4	5
Technological savvy	1	2	3	4	5
Marketing ability	1	2	3	4	5
Process knowledge	1	2	3	4	5
Industry experience	1	2	3	4	5
Physical stamina	1	2	3	4	5

By this stage, you should have a fair idea of both your competition's weaknesses and your own strengths. Craft your vision taking both—plus your values—into consideration. If very few competitors provide good customer service and your own people skills, communication skills, and management ability are outstanding, it makes sense to develop your vision focusing on customer service. If your knowledge of manufacturing processes and creative abilities are superior, your vision should include creating one of the best products in your industry.

Telling Everyone

Once you've opened the doors of your business, the next step will be to tell everyone what your vision of excellence is. Share it with the media, customers, and suppliers—and constantly to your own employees, who will carry out that vision.

Psychiatrist Howard Alt has seen Charlie Trotter in action during the nightly meeting he convenes prior to service. "Trotter stresses excellence in the food, the service, ambiance, and the wine program," says Alt. "Every employee learns Trotter's vision very quickly—what he expects and what he wants. He expects everybody to share that vision."

The chef-owner makes sure that the media doesn't miss out on his gospel, either. "I don't think Charlie for a minute, from the time he conceived it, thought he would do anything except have an operation that would be accepted internationally as a great restaurant," says *Chicago Tribune* food and wine columnist Bill Rice. How could Rice know that? Trotter knows that one of the best ways to attract coverage is through face-to-face contact, and he's spoken to the columnist on numerous occasions about his vision.

Invite local print, radio, and TV reporters to visit your store, factory, shop, or restaurant. Give them a tour of your operation and conclude with a press reception with hors d'oeuvres and drinks. Most important, tell them how you arrived at your vision and passionately express how much it means to you. Especially if your plans are ambitious ones, they'll be interested to hear what you have to say.

Whatever you do, don't forget to tell your customers. Superior product quality, service, and customer relations will certainly speak for themselves, but you should remind customers of your vision in company advertisements, newsletters, or brochures. You and your staff can also speak with customers regularly about where the company is heading during service interactions.

Describe your vision to vendors so they'll make sense of your unusually high standards, instead of thinking you're a crank. Explain that you cannot do business with suppliers who provide inferior products, but have something gracious to offer, as well. For example, host a cocktail party and invite your vendors to tour your operation to see how you work toward your vision. From day one, Charlie Trotter has articulated his vision to the operation's suppliers, from fishermen to wine makers to small-scale farmers, to foster a quality partnership. He knows it's wise to share the vision with vendors, since they control the quality of supply products, reliable and prompt delivery, and fair prices—all critical to excellence. As a result, they have a tangible understanding of it and no doubts about exactly what the master chef expects of them.

"Farmers hand-pick everything for us," says former Trotter's chef de cuisine Guillermo Tellez. "Many grow fruits and vegetables expressly for us. They know exactly what we want, picking the best produce for us. They know other restaurants will accept second best." Vendors send the finest because after years of experience supplying Trotter, they know he wouldn't have it any other way.

"Charlie is very clear on his vision for the restaurant and has no problem sharing that vision with anyone who will listen," Trotter controller Judi Carle says with a wry smile. "He talks about it with the staff on a daily basis. He shares it with the guests. He hammers it home to the press. And he shares it with friends. I've even heard him telling it to a cab driver."

Think Big,

Because There's Always Room at the Top

"This is a restaurant like Cape Canaveral is an airport," raves *Chicago* magazine, in a review of Charlie Trotter's. "Every new dish represents a journey into a hitherto unexplored culinary terrain." "Every detail is attended to," chimes in *Esquire*. Phil Vettel, *Chicago Tribune* food critic, agrees: "The final number? Four. That's how many stars this place deserves. I'd give it more, but that's all I have." Writes another: "Trotter is looking for culinary heaven. I don't think he's going to stop until he thinks he gets there." Today, Charlie Trotter's accolades tumble in left and right. But it wasn't always that way.

In 1987, twenty-seven-year-old Trotter, then a novice chef and an aspiring entrepreneur, set a tremendous goal for himself and his business: his operation would become an international dining destination, on par with the very finest he'd enjoyed in Europe. At the time, Chicago boasted only two or three nationally recognized fine eateries—all of them European owned and operated. When rookie Trotter let it be known he intended to best the competition, plenty of respected critics and industry observers thought the young chef was crazy. Who did this kid from Chicago's suburban Wilmette think he was, anyway?

Turned out he was a dreamer with an exceptional vision, along with the guts and determination to achieve it.

"To be independent of public opinion is the first formal condition for achieving anything great," wrote the German philosopher and social theorist G. W. F. Hegel. At college, where Charlie Trotter studied political science, he read the German theorist's words and took them to heart. Once he formed his master vision, he refused to be deterred by detractors. It's a lesson you, too, should take to heart.

WHEN ROOKIE TROTTER LET IT BE KNOWN HE INTENDED TO BEST THE COMPETITION, PLENTY OF RESPECTED CRITICS AND INDUSTRY OBSERVERS THOUGHT THE YOUNG CHEF WAS CRAZY. WHO DID THIS KID FROM CHICAGO'S SUBURBAN WILMETTE THINK HE WAS, ANYWAY? TURNED OUT HE WAS A DREAMER WITH AN EXCEPTIONAL VISION, ALONG WITH THE GUTS AND DETERMINATION TO ACHIEVE IT.

No matter where you're located, there's nothing worth doing short of trying to create the crème de la crème in your industry.

Today, the majority of new entrepreneurs are guilty of one unforgivable sin: harboring uninspiring goals and dreams. "All I want is to maintain a steady stream of business," you often hear. "It would be great if I could stay open for years." "I'd be satisfied if I could just make decent money." Such lukewarm aspirations produce middling results.

When Charlie Trotter comes up with an idea, he focuses on the big picture and doesn't stumble on the minutiae, his staff says. In 1996, Trotter decided to remodel the building adjacent to his restaurant and declared the space would be used for offices, for testing cookbook recipes, and to film a cooking show. "At that time we had no cooking show lined up," remembers Controller Judi Carle. "In fact, we hadn't discussed the idea in anything but cursory fashion." A year and a half later, however, not only was the remodel complete, but the cooking program was filmed and in postproduction. Says Carle, "Charlie was completely confident the entire time that we would work out the details. As usual, he was right."

Bold visionaries dare to dream big. They set out to be the very best at what they do, locally, nationally—even internationally. "You've got to have a really lofty vision. Goals that are perhaps even unrealistic," says Trotter.

Big dreams also mean planning big. Research is mandatory— but carrying it out need not be a terrible burden. For the interested, scores of guides to superior businesses already exist. An aspiring entrepreneur in the restaurant industry, for example, can consult a range of guides from Mobil, Frommer's, Zagat Guide, and AAA, to epicurean magazines such as *Gourmet, Food & Wine, Bon Appétit,* and *Wine Spectator.* For a more detailed financial analysis, the fledgling restaurateur might turn to trade publications such as *Restaurants & Institutions, Restaurant Hospitality, Food Arts,* and *Nation's Restaurant News* magazine. Every industry can claim parallel publications. Profiling successful (and failing) business ventures is the raison d'etre of broad-topic national business magazines such as *Fortune, Business Week,* and *Forbes.* The *New York Times, Wall Street Journal, Time, Newsweek,* and local and regional business publications also cover major business milestones as a matter of course.

Available at the public library and published annually, Gale Research's *Encyclopedia of Associations* lists active trade, business, and professional associations; briefly describes their activities; and lists their publications. Trade associations are also a good source for industry information, but be wary of rankings. Examine the methodology they use to compile lists of winners. If revenues or profits are the main factor used to define superiority, don't go by their definition. (The highest grossing Fortune 500 firm isn't necessarily an excellent one.)

After you've done your background research, call organizations such as the American Marketing Association, introduce yourself, and ask the executive director to recommend five operations around the country he or she considers to be superior. Next, ask five industry experts, from journalists to academic analysts, to name the five most exceptional businesses in your area of interest.

You should now have a valuable listing of superb companies in the particular industry you're in or that you plan to penetrate. Whether you're interested in retail clothing stores, bed-and-breakfasts, art galleries, car dealerships, or auto parts factories, make time to visit the businesses you've identified as excellent. Ask management if you can spend a day or more observing their operations. In fields such as the hospitality industry, you may be able to gather all the information you need as a traveler, a hotel guest, or a fine diner.

By all means, don't forget to bring your notepad and pencil. When you travel, observe customer service interactions at each business and take notes. How do associates approach customers? Describe their product knowledge, level of care, and attention to detail. What is it about their efforts that sets them apart from competitors? How do they go the extra mile for customers? How could you improve on what they do?

If they manufacture or process a product, how is it made? What is it about the raw materials that makes their product special? Describe their inspection process. What about their processes or systems makes their product special? Do they use any extraordinary techniques, methods, or technologies to make their products?

When it's possible to sit in on meetings or brainstorming sessions, observe how company leaders encourage innovation. Do they urge everyone to participate in the ideation process? How do they encourage contributions? When it comes to training employees, how much time and manpower do they invest? Who is responsible for it? Do they employ unorthodox training techniques?

Keep a discerning eye for design innovations, especially if you are in or plan to open a retail or hospitality business. Does the company you're observing invest a lot of money in design? Visit the site where day-to-day business transactions are carried out. Describe the feeling evoked in the space. Are there special touches that make the space extraordinary? How does the design reflect the business and its owner?

Finally, remember that there is no substitute for "real time" experience. To really get a good look at what these top businesses do, you're going to have to literally get involved in them. Offer to work for each firm at no cost for at least a full week. If this idea seems like a caprice or an adolescent fantasy, think again. As Trotter and his colleagues know from experience, *it pays off.* Indeed, there are few world-class chefs who have not put in slavelike stints at fine Parisian, Milanese, or New York City restaurants to learn the meaning of excellence in cooking. Trotter himself worked in more than twenty restaurants, from California to Florida and Illinois to New York, before he opened Charlie Trotter's.

While working or volunteering for the businesses you've identified as superior, ask leaders to define their vision and values. Notice how they implement them. Observe how their employees interact with one another and with customers. Keep your eyes open for unusual employee motivational techniques, intensive training systems, and outstanding customer service.

After investing your valuable time working at several excellent operations, you'll compare and contrast. Because you've actually experienced what separates excellent businesses from ordinary businesses, you can now attempt to compete on a national and possibly even international level. Get ready to synthesize this information and funnel the real prize. Keep that goal grand, because there's always room at the top.

your staff
(part i):

HIRING AND

TRAINING FOR

EXCELLENCE

Hire for Desire

Rather Than Experience

Hiring for excellence is a very serious exercise for which you should be well prepared. The one characteristic employees have to possess above all others is attitude, or what Charlie Trotter sometimes refers to as "fire and desire." An applicant with little or no experience but a burning desire to learn and be part of an excellent firm will be a better employee than a highly experienced or pedigreed slouch. "Attitude, attitude, and attitude are the three most important qualities," says Trotter. Think of a legal assistant who's not afraid to revise a document ten times to get it right, a truck driver willing to do anything to deliver baked goods fresh and on time, or a director of marketing willing to pitch in and answer the phones when the receptionist is sick. "I look for people who are psyched and ready to do whatever it takes," explains Trotter. "Attitude is about being on fire—you've got to approach work like it's a religious experience."

Playing Smart in the Résumé Game

In metropolitan areas such as New York or Chicago, employers frequently receive hundreds of résumés in response to help-wanted ads. To select and interview any more than five applicants is a colossal (but not uncommon) waste of time, so begin with a highly selective review of your applicants' cover letters and résumés. Ideally, you'll interview only three or four sufficiently qualified applicants who express an ardent desire to work for your company.

To select the small first round of candidates, Charlie Trotter's managers conduct an impromptu fifteen-minute phone interview to determine if applicants even approximate the restaurant's standards. Trotter's people are on the lookout for two attributes: burning desire and well-honed communication skills. Does the applicant sound lively and energetic? Why does he want to work for Trotter's? What excites her about the job? Is he passionate? Intelligent and comprehensible? Courteous and well mannered? Because this phone interview comes as a total surprise, potential employees are forced to "think on their feet" and are more natural than in a preplanned interview.

To be considered, applicants must be resourceful enough to go to a library and read several articles about your industry and your company in particular. They should know the name of the CEO or the director of the department to which they are applying. Don't waste time talking to job seekers who have no clue about your business. End the conversation quickly.

Once the select group of applicants makes the first cut, invite each person to come for an hour-long interview at your office. Prepare in advance a list of questions that will help you to understand each person's passion, personality, values, goals, and interests—in other words, what makes him or her tick. An hour-long interview might only allow you to ask a handful of questions, depending on how concise or detailed the candidate's answers are, so it's essential to go into it with a strategy if you hope to gain insight into the individual.

Whatever you do during the interviews, don't spend time reviewing points on their résumés: dig deep and find out why they are there. When Charlie Trotter speaks to applicants, his priority is to figure out exactly why they wish to work at his restaurant and why they believe they're suited for the position. He knows applicants have to really want to work at Charlie Trotter's to survive there. He has no tolerance for weak links in the chain; employees must be entirely devoted to the operation. To get at their motives, he asks candidates to describe their favorite job, where they prefer to dine, and why they prefer to dine there.

Observe the applicant carefully during the interview, keeping an eye on body language, poise, and facial expressions. The only applicants who should be considered are those who treat the interview process with proper respect. An interviewee who is not punctual, for instance, should be rejected immediately.

After you've asked your questions, it's time for you to explain your business, your vision, your demands, and your expectations. As Stanford University professor Jerry I. Porras and management educator James C. Collins write in the *Harvard Business Review* (Sept/Oct, 1996), "You must translate the vision from words to pictures with a vivid description of what it will be like to achieve your goal." Hammer home to applicants how your business aspires to surpass mediocre ones—and just what kind of sacrifices employees make to be part of it. Don't mince words. During an interview, out of polite convention if nothing else, nearly every job seeker will tell you he or she is eager to come on board. Those who don't have the right stuff know it, and once they're out the door, they quickly disappear.

Keep your eye on the clock. It's important to relate to applicants what it will be like to work for your company, but take no more than fifteen minutes to do it. Statistically, one of the biggest mistakes interviewers make is to spend 80 percent of an interview speaking about themselves and their company. Use the brief opportunity you have to find out about your employee and not as a showcase for your ego.

Even after a series of careful interviews, sometimes a new hire performs far better during the selection process (or on paper) than on the job. The fact is, to nail that job, many interviewees will tell you exactly what you want to hear. That's natural. They're trying to provide the best picture of themselves that they can. It's just not always an accurate one. To compound the problem, many former employers aren't always candid when asked for references. They fear legal retribution, they're lazy, or they're just too busy to remember clearly. So although you may already be fairly good at weeding out pretenders, occasionally a dud will slip through.

Another problem is mismatches. If yours is a business that sets extraordinary goals, inevitably a sizable portion of new employees will spend a day observing and find they simply don't belong there. For some, the work will be too intense; others may find it too monotonous, or too challenging, or too easy.

For these reasons, it's wise to have leading candidates undergo a period of observation, as they do at Trotter's by working at least two consecutive forty-hour weeks on a trial basis. The trial period gives you a realistic way to evaluate potential employees at work before you invest heavily in their training, while they can figure out whether they will be happy working for you.

Those who are currently employed elsewhere probably will only be able to work part-time, but they should still be asked to spend eighty hours or more during the week, weekends, or whenever they are able to work. Pay trial employees a competitive starting wage, and make sure your manager is there to observe their work.

"I LOOK FOR PEOPLE WHO ARE PSYCHED AND READY TO DO WHATEVER IT TAKES," EXPLAINS TROTTER. "ATTITUDE IS ABOUT BEING ON FIRE— YOU'VE GOT TO APPROACH WORK LIKE IT'S A RELIGIOUS EXPERIENCE."

At Trotter's, the observation process works beautifully as a self-elimination process as well. "For anybody who wants to work with Charlie Trotter, all you have to do is observe the restaurant in action for a minute and you know what it's going to take to work there," says long-time customer Dick Berger. "Not everyone is a Charlie Trotter's staff person. You need to be truly disciplined."

Trotter's candidates who consider "menial" tasks beneath them simply aren't hired. During a hiring period last November, for example, the restaurant was in the process of interviewing new servers. One chaotic night, an employee fell ill, and the team found itself short a bus person. The solution was clear: hire one of the new wait-staff applicants a night early, and have him pitch in and bus tables for the evening. Unfortunately, the selected candidate considered the bussing assignment a personal insult and refused to come in for that shift. As a result, his application for the waiter position was disposed of as well.

Extraordinary individuals, on the other hand, will see in your operation exactly the type of establishment they dream of working for. Says one top hostess: "When I observed for the second night, it was like theater in a way. It was so exciting to watch how so many different things come together. I was looking for something dramatic, special, individual. Trotter's was exactly what I wanted." When Trotter's managers hired her, they knew right away they had a match.

The observation period also provides an opportunity to test candidates' resourcefulness. Some entrepreneurs present applicants with customer-service scenarios to determine how they would handle difficult situations. At Charlie Trotter's, would-be kitchen employees are given the Mystery Basket Test. The challenge: several ingredients are placed on a tray and the applicant is told to prepare a four-course meal for the chef, sous chef, assistant sous chef, and the pastry chef—without time to consult cookbooks or peers.

During the period of observation, push candidates extra hard and scrutinize their performance throughout the day to be sure they're physically strong and mentally alert, upbeat, able to handle long hours, positive, good-humored, and excited about the work they're doing. Test their confidence. Create straightforward decision-making scenarios to determine whether candidates are comfortable taking action and if, when pressed, they're confident enough to stand by their own decisions. Self-assured employees can be counted on to make decisions quickly and well, saving you or your managers time and headaches down the road.

How to Brainwash Your Employees

and Supervise for Your Super Vision

As an employer, you've got an ideological task at hand: You've hired grade-A employees. Now it's time to brainwash them.

While Charlie Trotter can't recommend indoctrination by force—you might get arrested—he insists that as a leader you must consistently encourage your staff to share your values, strive for your vision, and believe any goal you set is achievable—up to and including international superiority.

Many employees come in with a gung-ho attitude, but few know how to deliver excellence consistently and continuously. Even the most eager people you hire will require reeducation. Indoctrination is no piece of cake. Many employees will not understand why they and the business need to continuously improve—especially if your firm has already been named one of the best in the field or had a record sales year. Very likely, most of your staff will think that "good enough" is actually good enough. Why? Because most people are simply striving to make an adequate living and keep up with the Joneses. But your job isn't to help them keep up with the Joneses, or anyone else. Your job is to make them think like you.

The key to indoctrination is verbal communication supported by positive and consistent action. According to you, what are integrity, commitment, and consistency? Your employees aren't going to comprehend your values unless you talk about them on a regular schedule, like clockwork. While this might seem obvious, many managers, leaders, and entrepreneurs rarely define or express their values at all.

This is not the case at Charlie Trotter's, where the chef talks about his vision relentlessly and fervently. Some days he speaks like a preacher, other times like a drill sergeant, sometimes like a coach. For the restaurant's employees, Trotter's vision—to do whatever it takes to consistently provide excellent food and wines, service, and atmosphere—is the only one that matters. Yet Trotter has a double challenge, since his vision includes food and service excellence, both of which are very hard to pinpoint. In a sense, in these areas, superiority is in the eyes of the beholder. So it's his job to define what they mean to him, day in and day out. At the end of the day, only his definition of excellent food or consistency counts.

Provide your own employees with examples of how values you find important are put into practice. With his restaurant staff, Charlie Trotter frequently refers to films, books, music, other businesses, and sports teams to provide examples. He'll recommend employees read Ayn Rand's *The Fountainhead* to better understand integrity and commitment. He'll point to the Chicago Bulls championship teams to illustrate hard work, dedication, consistency, and teamwork. To ver-

FOR THE RESTAURANT'S EM-PLOYEES, TROTTER'S VISION— TO DO WHATEVER IT TAKES TO CONSISTENTLY PROVIDE EX-CELLENT FOOD AND WINES, SERVICE, AND ATMOSPHERE— IS THE ONLY ONE THAT MAT-TERS. . . . AT THE END OF THE DAY, ONLY HIS DEFINITION OF EXCELLENT FOOD OR CONSIS-TENCY COUNTS.

ify that employees have a clear understanding of what he believes and wants for the business, Trotter asks them during meetings to cite in-house examples illustrating company values.

An exercise employees really enjoy is to discuss other companies or institutions that don't practice your company's values on a regular basis. You and your staff won't have much trouble listing twenty such examples, such as outrageous customer service transactions, defective products, ineffective marketing or advertising campaigns, weak theater performances, lousy dining experiences, and cab rides from hell. Together, analyze how specific values obviously were not taken into consideration.

Occasionally, your firm might drift away from its value-based moorings. One of the most vital roles you will play as leader and value shaper is to note organizational or companywide deviations from company principles. Perhaps, for example, there has been an unusually high number of product returns or customer complaints regarding service. You need to express your disapproval, and do so in terms of your values.

Positive reinforcement is as key to maintaining values as is citing deviations. Celebrate and publicly congratulate staff members when they put your values into practice—those who go the extra mile, work long hours, perform tasks they're not expected to, execute work consistently, and continuously improve. Make sure they know how much you appreciate adherence to these principles.

What will really convince your employees you believe strongly in these values is to not stray from them: no one is going to take you seriously if you say you believe strongly in diligence and hard work but spend most of your time vacationing in Florence or Raratonga. Similarly, if you purchase shoddy equipment and allow inferior products to be shipped to customers, employees will know you can't possibly be serious about integrity and high standards. You have to be the standard-bearer and lead by example.

Because you're human, you might occasionally slip and do something that's inconsistent with your values. When you do, the most humble, courageous (and clever) thing you can do is to acknowledge your lapse. Doing so instills trust in your fair judgment and sends a message that you practice what you preach.

Though employees might provide innovative ideas to help you to strive for the vision, in the final analysis the company vision is yours. You need to persuade them to put aside their visions and definitions of excellence and embrace yours. They can have their own visions when they start their own businesses.

Supervision for Your Super Vision

Once you've brainwashed your employees, how do you ensure that your indoctrination sticks—even when the going gets rough? As the leader of a dynamic outfit, you'll need to guarantee excellent output and service even amidst a riot of activity. Here, one can definitely take a cue from Chef Trotter.

The best way for you to ensure that employees strive for excellence is to supervise them closely day in and day out. Although Charlie Trotter speaks about his company's vision constantly and provides concrete examples to help his staff understand what he requires, evangelism is not nearly enough. Trotter and his managers must constantly monitor employee behavior and modify it when it isn't consistent with his vision.

Many businesses scrutinize staff performance only once a year during employee reviews. Problem is, old habits die hard. Employees who are allowed to compromise the company's principles for any length of time will not easily change. In businesses like Charlie Trotter's, where excellence is paramount, staff reviews take place on a regular basis. That way, employees know at all times exactly where they stand and how they need to improve.

Create an evaluation form for you or your managers to formally assess employee performance at monthly intervals. Managers should be evaluated as well. Providing constant, instantaneous feedback is essential for shaping and molding each employee, especially following major departures from company values. A more regular, formal process, however, allows you to track employee progress over time.

To get started, refer to the list of values that you have decided are most important to you after completing the exercises in Lesson 2 (page 11). Then identify several aspects of each principle you wish to address and set them up on a scale. These will help pinpoint manager and employee adherence to the vision. Keep the form simple so it can be completed quickly and easily. Here's a sample:

Employee Name _____ Date _____

Evaluated by _____

Evaluate the employee on a scale of 1 (disagree strongly) to 5 (agree strongly)

Consistency
   1) Work is of high quality daily   1   2   3   4   5
   2) Works with same intensity daily   1   2   3   4   5
   3) Is consistently positive and enthusiastic   1   2   3   4   5
   4) Does what s/he promises to do   1   2   3   4   5

Dedication
   1) Reports to work early and stays late   1   2   3   4   5
   2) Takes on extra work to learn and grow   1   2   3   4   5
   3) Strongly believes in the company vision   1   2   3   4   5

Diligence
   1) Is not afraid of difficult work   1   2   3   4   5
   2) Applies her/himself completely every day   1   2   3   4   5
   3) Goes to any length to complete work   1   2   3   4   5

Perseverance
   1) Sticks with difficult work until it's done   1   2   3   4   5
   2) Undeterred by internal or external obstacles   1   2   3   4   5
   3) Persists even when success seems unlikely   1   2   3   4   5

After a monthly evaluation is conducted, it's time for managers to share the information with employees—one-on-one and privately, in a fifteen-minute review.

Present all the information in terms of your vision and values and help to find solutions. You might say: "I've noticed over the past month you haven't worked with the same level of intensity every day. What's holding you back? Is something wrong? Are you getting enough rest?"

Don't forget to mention how well the individual is performing and in which specific areas. Identify exceptionally good work and encourage it through rewards or praise. In Charlie Trotter's preservice meetings, Trotter frequently commends employees for a particularly astute choice or move the previous evening. Doing so teaches the rest of the team what it takes to deliver excellence.

Besides monitoring employee adherence to your company's values, you need to monitor job- and task-related fundamentals, too. Every business has essential chores—from the menial to the glamorous—that need to be completed on deadline. The easiest way to ensure they are completed perfectly is to create a checklist with codified tasks.

"Every front-of-the-house employee at Trotter's has a setup sheet when they walk in the front door each day," explains Director of Operations Mitchell Schmieding. "At the beginning of the shift, I'm standing next to the sign-off sheet, checking to see if every task is done. If it's not done right, they're going to hear from me."

Some aspects of quality service, however, can't be codified on a checklist. Even after you've taught your staff how to deliver stellar service and tested their knowledge to your satisfaction, you'll need to observe them in action. At Trotter's, managers are responsible for making sure floor staff have significant product knowledge—about wine and food ingredients—and that they share it with customers. Managers must also see to it that employees address customers by name and are warm, courteous, and attentive, yet not too intrusive or familiar. In short, they insure that the staff consistently make customers happy. Indeed, one of management's primary responsibilities during dinner service is to keep their ears and eyes open to spot poor service.

Some of you will have no problem expressing your displeasure in a fair but firm manner. Others are somewhat inhibited, worried their employees will quit if they are too hard on them or simply afraid to hurt anyone's feelings. Yet if your ideal is excellence, it can't be emphasized enough that you correct mistakes *immediately*. The more times an action is performed incorrectly, the more difficult it is to correct. Why? At Trotter's, experience shows that failing to regularly correct sloppiness, carelessness, or attitude problems becomes a tacit endorsement or acceptance of these behaviors.

Whatever you do, don't mince words. Make sure employees know you're displeased when you correct their behavior. If an unacceptable type of behavior is repeated, such as unexplained or regular absences, it's your job to explain to individuals the consequences, up to and including dismissal.

For practical and legal as well as ethical reasons, never attack staff members personally—meaning an insult to an employee's intelligence, personality, or appearance. Criticisms should always focus on the *act* rather than the *person*. Calling someone an idiot, for example, is not only crude and childish, but may also elicit a lawsuit that could close the doors of your business. Instead, tailor admonitions to each person's disposition and personality. A thick-skinned, wise-cracking cook may take a harder ribbing in good stead, whereas the sweet-natured and shy busboy may fall apart under the same harsh words. In all cases, it's best to follow criticisms with reminders that individual contributions are essential to the business's success.

Employees will never take you seriously if you correct them but don't provide solutions or concrete examples of the proper way to perform a task. The "I just don't like it when you do it" line is not going to fly. Nor will the "Because I said so" explanation stick. Say that an employee, when asked by a customer, has scanty knowledge of the salmon terrine, health equipment, or 900-megahertz cordless phones your company sells—and your knowledge is also limited. Don't criticize. Suggest books to read, manuals to research, videos to watch, products to sample, and peers to consult.

Most important, provide the underlying reasons why, according to your company's philosophy, a skill or procedure must be followed. Explain, for example, that product knowledge is a critical component of service—customers expect service staff who intimately know the products they're offering—and that exceptional service is key to the vision. This way, the employee is more likely to appreciate and respect the criticism.

Get to Know Your Employees

One of the business world's pet concepts several years ago was MBWA—Management by Walking Around. The theory held that senior managers should spend a good portion of their days strolling around factory floors and corporate offices, "pressing the flesh" with employees. Staff, it followed, would be strongly motivated by superiors who demonstrated they were "part of the gang" and concerned about their employees' well-being.

The concept is fine. But this lesson asks you to take the MBWA strategy beyond mere posturing—and really get to know your employees. Because you hired them based on stringent criteria, they will very likely be passionate, intelligent, and hard-working, with exceptional energy and sound values. You'll have to go deeper and find out what makes each of your employees tick if you want a vibrant, stable workforce that continuously strives for excellence.

Unfortunately, most employees in both large and small businesses are rarely asked how they're doing or what's going on in their lives—unless they're frequently late to work, their performance is inconsistent, or they seem troubled. In most American workplaces, they've come to expect an utter lack of interest on the part of management. Alienation grows. Production and quality suffer.

Western Airlines' CEO knew this and spent hours "in the trenches" with everyone from company baggage handlers to pilots. After personally familiarizing himself with slews of workers and the tasks they performed, the CEO was able to convince employees to accept cuts in pay in exchange for ownership stake. With this and other moves, he made Western so secure financially that it sold to Delta for $680 million.

The story doesn't end there. After the corporate sale, Delta's CEO subsequently cut the workforce by one-third and treated the remaining employees so harshly that the airline's famed customer service

ABOVE ALL, LET EMPLOYEES KNOW THROUGH YOUR SINCERE ACTIONS THAT YOU CARE ABOUT THEIR LIVES, THEIR FAMILIES, AND THEIR CONCERNS. IT'S THE SMARTEST INVESTMENT YOU CAN POSSIBLY MAKE IN HUMAN RESOURCES, BECAUSE YOUR EMPLOYEES WILL CARE MORE ABOUT YOUR CONCERNS, PARTICULARLY YOUR VISION OF EXCELLENCE.

vanished. In the process, droves of talented administrators fled to other firms. By 1997, the Delta CEO admitted that he had made a colossal mistake. Not surprisingly, he was given his walking papers by the board of directors.

Spending Time with Your Employees

One of the methods Charlie Trotter frequently uses to get to know his employees is to take them on business trips to assist him. Since, on most of these excursions, they're not actually working the entire time, Trotter has a good opportunity to see what his employees are really like: what they like to eat, how they like to dress, what kind of music they listen to, what leisure activities they prefer. Consequently, he becomes closer with many of these individuals. It's a lot easier, Trotter knows, to spend many hours together trying to build an excellent business with employees you genuinely like than with employees you merely tolerate. And you can't possibly like people you don't really know.

"In a business like mine, I think it is essential to like your employees," admits Trotter. Gone are the days, he says, when employees were thought of as mere office or production-line automatons whose emotions were irrelevant to company goals. We now know better. "If I owned a company with fifty outlets and several thousand employees, I couldn't possibly know them all," Trotter continues. "But it is crucial to like your employees when you have one outlet and fifty employees."

More than anything, as company head you need to know whether your employees are happy or not. Why? Unhappy employees irritate customers, demotivate their coworkers, and don't perform to the best of their ability. Simply put, it's impossible to work with unhappy people. Long-term effects? Unhappy individuals quit. If they're valuable employees, you don't want that to happen with any regularity. No business can take such repeated shocks and endure.

Discontent is not always resolvable. Some individuals are chronically miserable because they're mismanaging their own personal lives. Often, their work suffers from it. In such cases, warn the employee and explain that he or she will need to address an unhappy personal situation because work performance has been poor, careless, or inconsistent. Those unable to change must be dismissed with a written explanation citing breaches in performance or reliability.

While some individuals will never be happy, a larger number are discontented for work-related reasons. Your job is to observe employees every day and ask your managers to also monitor employee satisfaction. (The overtly miserable are easy to spot, because they complain on a fairly regular basis. You must also keep an eye out for less demonstrative types, who allow their unhappiness to mount up inside, then suddenly quit.)

If you detect several individuals who seem unhappy, call them aside and let them know you would like to ask them some questions in a group setting (they'll be more communicative in a group than in a one-on-one meeting). Once the group has gathered, explain that you'd like each person to be entirely candid so you can enhance employee satisfaction. Find out how they feel about their place of work, their positions, their coworkers, and you. If you have a hunch about the source of discontent, ask direct questions.

- **About the company:** What do you like about this company? What do you dislike? Is everyone given the tools and support they need? Do you believe the company is fair and responsive to its employees and customers? If not, why? Is the culture what you expected? Are you proud of the work we do or what we accomplish? If not, why? Do you like working with our customers? How would you describe the physical appearance and layout? The company benefits? What could the company do to make this a better place to work? What could you do to make it better?

- **About the job:** How is your work going? What do you enjoy about your work? What do you dislike? Describe your workload. Do you believe you were trained well for the position? What would you change? Are you supervised too much or not enough? Do you believe you have enough organizational support and the proper technology and equipment to do your job? What would you suggest? How would you describe your work space or office? Do you believe you're compensated fairly? What could the company do to make your job more rewarding? What could you do to make your job more enjoyable?

- About the boss: Candidly, do you feel I'm fair and reasonable? Am I understanding? Am I in touch with the needs of employees and the day-to-day work? Am I available to you? Am I consistent? How would you describe your relationship with me? What could I do to improve our relationship? What could you do to improve our relationship?

When you take the time to go to such lengths, your employees will very likely approve of your attempts to be thoughtful and proactive. They'll be far more impressed if you then act upon the areas of concern that they expressed. With direct employee input, determine which concerns or complaints should be solved immediately, which can wait, and which are actually invalid. (Certainly, when a number of employees are disgruntled for the same reason—for example, outdated technical tools—it's essential to resolve the problem immediately.)

To further open lines of communication, create casual, conversational situations that inspire your employees to open up and be themselves. You might begin by talking to them about your childhood, family life, education, sports activities, or non-work-related hobbies, as well as dining experiences and travels. Encourage them to talk about theirs. Invite them to lunch or dinner at a restaurant or at your home. Observe how they interact with coworkers. Are they particularly witty, caustic, artistic, good-humored, analytical, romantic, reserved, mechanical, or compassionate? Encourage frequent employee outings. Above all, let employees know through your sincere actions that you care about their lives, their families, and their concerns. It's the smartest investment you can possibly make in human resources, because your employees will care more about *your* concerns, particularly your vision of excellence.

With a better understanding of their personalities, character traits, and interests, you'll be better able to train, coach, advance, and reward workers effectively. If they see themselves as your friend as well as your employee, they'll work harder for you, too. Creating this environment can be a challenge—most employees are more relaxed and comfortable around coworkers than around "the boss"—but the results in worker job satisfaction (and, hence, productivity) will reward your efforts.

Build Teams 9

Back in the 1980s, the Chicago Bulls were little more than a mediocre basketball club. Despite the presence of the miraculous Michael Jordan, the Bulls remained an organization of individuals, not a true team. By decade's end, the club was floundering, and the Bulls' management finally faced facts, realizing they needed to build a solid team. Signing on coach Phil Jackson to do just that, they became one of the best basketball clubs of all time.

Moral of the story? No matter how many stars you employ, organizational excellence will elude you if you refuse to build strong employee-based teams.

Perhaps, like many entrepreneurs, you aren't completely sold on the idea. For several years you've heard the stock phrase "teamwork" intoned religiously, the slogan "do it for the team" ad nauseam. Sounds fine, but you're just not convinced that individuals working in groups are any more productive or efficient than when they are working independently.

Your skepticism is quite reasonable. Most companies echo "pro-team" axioms regularly but don't create environments where teamwork is essential to departmental and organizational excellence. Furthermore, too many so-called "teams" have no clear goals or incentives to excel as a group. Consequently, individual members quickly begin "looking out for Number One," i.e., themselves—and anyone who doesn't ends up a patsy. Your task will be to develop entirely different kinds of teams that look out for group members and your organization above all.

There are very good motives for doing so. Well-built teams are able to accomplish more than great performers working independently. First, they capitalize on member strengths and minimize the impact of individual weaknesses. Second, members automatically evaluate each other's performance and contribution to the team, which drives individuals to work harder and more effectively than they might otherwise. Third, team employees often stick together when threatened by adversity or external forces.

In Charlie Trotter's company "culture," emphasis is placed on successful completion of any given

IN EXCELLENT BUSINESSES, EMPLOYEES ARE EXPECTED TO WORK FOR THE GOOD OF THE OPERATION, RATHER THAN TO ACHIEVE PERSONAL PROMINENCE OR SUCCESS. WHEN THE TEAM WINS, EVERYBODY WINS, AND IT'S YOUR JOB TO CONVINCE EMPLOYEES OF THAT FACT.

group task, rather than on determining which individual gets credit for it. As a result, staff members feel remarkably comfortable asking for help from others. Among its fifty employees, the restaurant has three official team groupings—in management, kitchen, and front of the house. Other, much less formal teams form as situations arise. A temporary team may be put together to handle a culinary exchange or a business trip, with each member responsible for a different angle. On a recent trip to San Francisco to give a cooking demonstration and cook a large-scale dinner, Trotter's team included one "point-person" who made travel arrangements and contacts with clients in California; another individual who saw that food was ordered, prepped, and packed; and a third who was responsible for assembling and packing fragile table decorations, books, and posters.

In excellent businesses, employees are expected to work for the good of the operation, rather than to achieve personal prominence or success. When the team wins, everybody wins, and it's your job to convince employees of that fact. That also means you need to remind employees to lend a helping hand when they have time and a coworker is overwhelmed, even when that person is a member of another team or department. At Trotter's, it is not a server's *primary* responsibility to bus tables or the chef's to wash dishes, but it becomes their responsibility when there's a crunch. Guests expect to be served world-class food and wine in a reasonably timely fashion, and they don't care whether their table is cleared by the person who's assigned to that station or by another who happens to be free to troubleshoot.

Composing a Team
To foster cohesiveness, build small teams of five to ten people. In these smaller groupings, individuals interact constantly, learn each others' strengths and weaknesses better, and are more likely to understand how each member's contributions affect the team's per-

formance. Plus, members of smaller teams are more likely to trust each other and become friends who'll stand by one another when the going gets tough.

It's a good idea to form one or more teams of individuals from a variety of departments, too. The best example of interdepartmental groups are management teams comprised of a manager from every department and you, the employer. Ask your managers to report to the group in a weekly meeting their team's progress and accomplishments, innovative solutions to problems, their team's concerns and perceptions regarding other teams, and any morale- and management-related concerns or problems. Collectively, the management team sets goals and directs strategies for the company.

It's best to form "quality circles." Essentially, groups of employees from a variety of departments, rather than managers, are assigned to gather in a weekly or monthly meeting to evaluate production, service, or efficiency problems. Quality circle members bring expertise and knowledge of their departments and functions to the table and look out for the organization as a whole. If, for example, the sales department has been losing accounts, the quality circle would gather to pinpoint the source of the problem, such as poor customer service, defective merchandise, or late shipments, and find solutions.

Now that you know what kinds of teams you need to organize, here are some surefire team-building tips:

- When you've got a good thing, leave it that way; the best way to foster tight-knit groups is to leave them intact as long as possible. Why? When a member leaves the group, voluntarily or not, it's often destablizing. It takes a good deal of time and diverted energy to bring a replacement up to speed on group norms and practices—enough so that that a new member can truly pull his or her own weight. All of these problems undermine group cohesiveness and effectiveness.

- Set aside time every month for teams to convene and set goals for themselves. In a companywide meeting, explain to employees the

purpose of the team meetings and allow them to schedule a convenient time to meet. Ask them to collectively set goals to improve their
team's attendance, productivity, customer service, sales, accuracy, efficiency—you name it. It's also smart to encourage teams to distribute
tasks or responsibilities among individual team members, based on
talents and knowledge. Who knows better what individual team members can accomplish?

Use the Carrot, Forget the Stick: Giving Rewards and Recognition

Now that we've sung the praises of a team-based workforce, let's
come down to earth and discuss the challenges you'll face.

Often, teams are not as demanding of themselves as you are of
them. So even though you've asked them to set their own goals,
you'll also need to set hard-to-reach, clear, and specific targets for
each team and explain what it will take to get there. Each year, for
example, Charlie Trotter asks his service team to shoot for the James
Beard Foundation's award for the best service in the nation. Equally
important, Trotter specifies for them on a daily basis what it will
take to reach the goal and provides concrete examples from other
great service businesses. The results so far? In the last five years, the
restaurant's service staff has been nominated for the prize five times.

In many firms, stellar individual job performances are frequently recognized in the form of "employee of the month" citations.
It's also important to honor teams as a unit. At Charlie Trotter's,
when the kitchen performs with exceptional skill, the chef publicly
recognizes and congratulates the entire team, rather than individual
members. Group recognition reinforces the importance of the team
to organizational excellence: all the players take great pride in being
a member of the group, while top performers realize they couldn't do
it without their entire team. As a side benefit, it also causes individuals who loaf to feel guilty and buck up, after being congratulated
for something they don't deserve.

In the professional sports arena, awards for individual accomplishments are rarely considered as prestigious as the team championship. As a matter of fact, Most Valuable Player status is almost always conferred to an outstanding player on a winning or contending team, because in the overall scenario it matters little how great a player is when his or her team doesn't win games.

Determine which performance measures are most important for the organization and reward teams accordingly—usually with money or benefits. Depending on the nature of your business, a team might be rewarded for anything from accuracy to productivity to quality of workmanship. At Charlie Trotter's, the chef rewards the kitchen staff collectively for quality, attention to detail, accuracy, and efficiency measures, rather than volume or speed. A sales team might be rewarded for revenues generated, plus customer satisfaction. Whatever the criteria, team accolades encourage a collective push toward excellence.

Stellar Service Results from Stellar Training

There's a saying among restaurateurs: great service can compensate for mediocre fare, but great food can never make up for mediocre service. Indeed, in most businesses, quality service is just as important as product quality—or is more so.

"For the majority of our clients, service is the aspect that makes or breaks the experience," says Charlie Trotter's director of operations, Mitchell Schmieding. "The service staff can turn a merely pleasurable experience into something totally spectacular." Perhaps more critical, incompetent service staff can turn a lovely evening into a total disaster.

Dell Computers is a high-tech company consistently given highest marks for customer service—a fact that is fundamental to that company's success in the computer hardware industry, where a PC is, basically, a PC. It's no coincidence that Dell's stock has gone up fifteen-fold in the last two years. Dell's customer service representatives create an atmosphere of familiarity and connection to the company that has panned out in the form of increased investments.

No matter what business you're in, an excellent service record begins with great customer service training. Stellar service doesn't necessarily imply that you have to have Charlie Trotter's–style polish and sophistication—you'll define what appropriate-yet-professional service is for your business's atmosphere, and train your employees accordingly. What stellar service does have to do, however, is to add something special to the customer's experience.

Customers need to feel comfortable in your place of business. One way to be sure they do is to hire service staff people that "speak their language." What does that entail? Ask yourself: Is my clientele primarily young, middle-aged, or mature? Urban or rural? Hip or traditional? Then teach your employees to use appropriate language to address those customers. If you lack the social skills or cultural background to gauge what's right for your business, ask for tips from people who more closely match the demographics of your customers.

Each niche has a dialect all its own. If you serve affluent, refined clientele, your employees will obviously need to address customers in a more formal fashion. On the other hand, if you own a music store catering to customers mostly in their teens and twenties, your staff may freely and effectively use slang terms like "phat," "fly," and "the dope"—whether you understand them or not.

Employees are part actors and must also learn to "perform." You'll instinctively know to instruct employees to keep from horsing around or joking constantly in an elegant atmosphere. Believe it or not, you might also have to remind service staff in a more casual business atmosphere to have fun, relax, and refrain from being too somber.

Knowing the Product Intimately

Though the type of service differs from company to company, several elements of stellar service are universal to all businesses. Product knowledge is critical to great customer service. At Trotter's, servers are assigned a menu course, such as a fish course, and every day they are expected to research how the always-different dish was made, what ingredients it contains, where the ingredients are from, and how the dish tastes. Each server is then expected to share their knowledge with the rest of the floor staff at a daily preservice meeting.

"Our weekly wine meeting used to feature the sommelier—the wine steward—lecturing on different varieties week after week. So we changed it," Schmieding says. "I bought each team member a *Sotheby's Encyclopedia of Wine*. Now, I ask a different team member every week to prepare a presentation for the entire staff on a particular subject. They submit an outline a few days in advance of our weekly meetings; management reviews it and asks them to investigate issues they haven't covered before the presentation." As a result, the entire staff is involved in the training process, and employees come to rely on one another for answers and support.

It's also smart to allow your staff to sample or test your company's products or services, or offer them a deep discount to purchase merchandise. For years car dealers have given or loaned their sales staff people company cars to better acquaint them with their stock vehicles' handling, acceleration, styling, and special features. Similarly, shoe and clothing salespeople often own and wear the products they sell in the store so they can better describe the feel and fit. This tactic not only strengthens employee product knowledge, but also offers employees a handsome perk and inspires loyalty to the product.

"When a customer asks employees questions about a wine or food product, we don't want them giving a textbook description, but what they really think," says Schmieding. "We want them to knowledgeably recommend products." Monitor your staff's service transactions to ensure knowledge is expressed with respect. Condescending service can be the ultimate turn-off.

After employees have had the opportunity to study, sample, and talk about the products or services, give them an exam periodically to test their knowledge of such things as product characteristics, prices, and warranties. Based on their performances, you'll learn who knows your products inside and out, who needs help, and who's not doing their work. Employees lacking intimate knowledge of the product should not be in contact with customers.

"OUR STAFF INCLUDES A LOT OF PEOPLE WHO ARE INTELLIGENT, THAT REALLY GET WHAT WE'RE TRYING TO DO, AND ARE TRULY WILLING TO GIVE SOMETHING FROM THE HEART. THEIR MIND-SET IS, 'THERE'S NO SUCH THING AS THE WORD 'NO.' ' WHATEVER YOU CAN DO TO BLOW SOMEONE'S MIND—YOU GO FOR IT."

— Charlie Trotter

Besides a knowledge of warranty or discount policies, your staff needs to be armed with the other often-overlooked fundamentals, such as how to contact customer information quickly and easily, how to contact other departments, and where other branches of your business are located.

Giving Customers What They Need

Teach employees to be attentive and anticipate customer needs. Train your employees to spot customers who look lost or confused and offer to provide directions or information. Have them keep their eyes open at all times. When a customer needs assistance, ask employees to drop what they're doing if they're not with a customer or find a teammate who has time. At Trotter's, service employees are reminded to be always mindful of what's going on around them. That way, they'll be aware of the inquiring look on a guest's face or the napkin that's fallen to the floor, which can be replaced before the customer even notices it.

While you want your staff to attend to every customer need, you need to train them not to be intrusive or too friendly. There's nothing worse than the salesperson who won't leave you alone to browse. Teach your employees never to interrupt conversations, linger for great lengths of time, touch customers, or joke incessantly.

Instruct employees to never make excuses and never, ever blame the customer—no matter who is at fault. It's best to apologize, accept the blame, and offer to make the situation right. When a customer has a medium-rare New York steak in mind, for example, he doesn't care why the steak is well-done. If he accidentally asked for a well-done steak, it's fruitless for the waiter to "make the customer wrong." To lessen your staff's natural tendency to do so, empower employees to do whatever it takes to make customers happy. In the retail business, sales people may accept a return without a receipt under some circumstances, and hosts may offer a glass of champagne or canapé to a customer who's waited half an hour to be seated. When service is at stake, you must allow employees to use their judgment.

More important, you need to stand by their decisions. A story out of Nordstrom sales lore tells of an elderly woman who once came into the upscale clothing store to return auto tire chains. She insisted she'd purchased them there—despite the fact that Nordstrom doesn't sell anything faintly resembling the product. Instead of simply dismissing the shopper, however, the Nordstrom clerk did a little research. Discovering that the old woman was a long-time customer, he decided it wasn't wise to convince the woman she was "wrong." Instead, he called a nearby auto supply store to obtain a fair price and issued a sales credit to the woman. Having been told countless times by store supervisors to take care of the customer by any means necessary, the clerk was confident he wouldn't be fired for his choice. He guessed right. Nordstom's policy put stellar service before almost any other goal.

That's the way customer service must be approached, agrees Charlie Trotter:

> Our staff includes a lot of people who are intelligent, that really get what we're trying to do, and are truly willing to give something from the heart. Their mindset is, "There's no such thing as the word 'no.'" Whatever you can do to blow someone's mind—you go for it. Working the dining room floor is like a very complicated game of chess. You're thinking of strategic moves: services to perform on behalf of the guests—before they even ask for those things. It's the art of understanding, figuring out, and ascertaining what the expectations are for each and every table—and then exceeding those expectations. Even if those expectations are awesome.

Cross-Training Isn't Just for Athletes

When all-star athletes enter into training, they don't simply practice their own game. Their coaches know that cross-trained athletes have better coordination, strength, and stamina than those who train in only one discipline. The same holds true in the workplace: cross-trained employees will be more "fit" than their one-dimensionally trained counterparts.

You're probably thinking that it is expensive to train an employee to perform a variety of job functions, when all you need him to do is, say, file reports, answer phones, and enter data on a computer. Sure, cross-training is more expensive. What you end up with, though, is an employee of incalculably greater value to your organization. Think of it as an investment in the company's future.

Furthermore, cross-training teaches employees to respect one another's jobs and the amount of effort, skill, perseverance, concentration, and stamina required to perform each of them. Without that understanding, employees don't work well together and the company doesn't function at its best.

Trotter employee Michael Lutes had worked as a sous chef—or second-in-command—for a slew of celebrated restaurants around the country prior to coming to Charlie Trotter's. Cross-training at the celebrated Chicago restaurant meant veteran chef Lutes had to work his way back up the ladder—starting out in canapé, making tiny hors d'oeuvres—followed by lengthy stints at several kitchen stations. With his considerable culinary knowledge and expertise, was Lutes angry and resentful at being shifted about to less prestigious positions? "I was a sous chef, so starting from scratch took a lot of humility," admits Lutes. "But canapé was very good training. It really helps you gain the 'touch,' because the hors d'oeuvres are so small; you really have to be right on." Thanks to cross-training, Lutes says he was able to hone a sense of finesse and attention to detail. He realized that Trotter had envisioned him in a higher spot soon enough, but wanted to train him in all disciplines to make him that much more effective.

Trotter is an avid basketball fan, and he has learned from the game. Professional sports teams rehearse plays and practice them for weeks, but when the game starts, sometimes a player is hurt. Like a veteran coach, Charlie Trotter knows the best prepared team can make substitutions quickly, seamlessly, and successfully. In these support and substitution situations, cross-trained employees are invaluable. When an employee is sick or a colleague needs assistance or backup, a trained employee can come to the rescue where a novice cannot. The multitrained worker can actually sense when a colleague is overwhelmed. "At Charlie Trotter's, we rotate positions and let employees feel what each other staff member feels," explains Mitchell Schmieding. "There is a lot of stress and a lot of pressure here every night. I tell the staff this is like the Olympics. Every time you falter or miss a jump, our customers subtract a tenth of a point. Everybody has to give 100 percent, all the time." Workers understand the importance of each role only when they've actually worked in several posts.

In many industries or businesses, one function cannot be performed until another function is properly completed. Employees who have been trained to perform more than one function are more likely to be conscious of how their role fits into the big picture of the company. They know that if they screw up they will cause a bottleneck that might affect the entire organization. An added plus: it's a lot harder to loaf when the whole cross-trained crew knows whether people are pulling their weight or not.

The most effective cross-training allows employees to "feel the pain" of their coworkers—particularly colleagues with whom they'll need to work with in the future. In a first-class supermarket, for example, cashiers would put in stints as baggers, and vice versa. The result? Less grumbling, conflict, and slowdowns. Employees better understood what their coworkers had to deal with to get the job done.

In the restaurant industry, where animosity between front-house and kitchen employees is notorious—and corrosive—fostering empathy among workers may spell the difference between a tense atmosphere or a fine dining experience. Traditionally, kitchen employees complain that the waitstaff make mountains of money for little work and cushy hours; waiters often resent the kitchen crew, whom they see as insulated from the caprices of demanding customers. At Charlie Trotter's, there's no place for such a standoff, so waitstaff employees rotate among several positions in the kitchen, and kitchen employees work in the front of the house. Along the way, Trotter's staff members come to understand how hard each department works to make the evening a success, as well as the interdependence of departments and job functions.

Cross-training also keeps longtime staff members engaged and motivated. With new goals to reach and new challenges to overcome constantly, employees are less likely to be bored. Because cross-training means employees develop a variety of skills, your staff will also be better prepared to assume managerial positions in the future. How? Cross-trained workers know the length of time required to complete tasks. They're familiar with the "ins and outs"—the resources required, obstacles to performance, the stress factors. As tomorrow's managers, they'll also be more respected than supervisors who only know the job in theory. Cross-training rotations are also a great way to let an employee who has been entertaining the idea of a permanent transfer to a new department test the waters before taking the plunge.

Once you're convinced cross-training is vital to excellence, you need to take a number of steps to get the ball rolling. Even though cross-training is in both the employer's and employee's best interests, the latter won't see it that way. In fact, they're likely to view it as an imposition. Remain steadfast. Inform your current employees—including managers—that they will be cross-trained to perform several functions and will substitute for coworkers who are sick, have resigned, or have been terminated.

Explain the cross-training program to new hires *before* they accept a job. If you intend to hire a new recruit with ten years' sales experience, she needs to know she'll first be working in inventory for six months. Conversely, previous experience should not exempt new employees from intensive cross-training in their area of "expertise." Even highly experienced employees must learn from scratch how each department performs its work—and even more important, how it interfaces with the organization as a whole.

Before you institute a cross-training program, have a list of clear objectives—whether your aim is to reduce turnover, increase product knowledge or productivity, or prepare employees to become future managers.

The person best suited to train employees will often be the department's best performer. A leading salesperson or the most meticulous administrative assistant probably knows the job better than anyone. Yet not every departmental champion is a good, patient teacher. Some employees perform their jobs expertly but are unable to convey information to a trainee. If that's the case, the department supervisor might be better suited to train rotating employees, though even the finest supervisors are not aware of every small task or function their charges perform on the job. Indeed, for nuts-and-bolts descriptions of each job, no one is a more valuable source of information than the individual occupying that particular position. Ask every employee working each position to write a list of functions—even the seemingly insignificant—that he or she performs over the course of a month. That way, when it comes time to teach someone to perform the job, there will be written documentation outlining exactly what needs to get done.

The time needed to train employees really depends on the work at hand. While tasks such as filing, answering phones, or processing orders may take only a couple of weeks to learn, more complicated job skills—say, in brand management or sales—will probably take three to six months to learn. The quickest way to determine training time needed? Observe and talk to your employees.

While common sense should dictate how many job rotations are necessary to cross-train employees, it's safe to say it's unnecessary to cross-train employees in more than four functions. Bloomingdale's, for example, doesn't need to train sales clerks in every one of its departments, then also train them in accounting, marketing, finance, and public relations. But excellent stores do train customer service employees in two or three retail departments.

Test the success of your cross-training program every six months. Have both managers and trainees evaluate the program through written questionnaires, and test their performance and product knowledge with oral and written exams. The final story is in the numbers: measure increases in sales, quality of service, speed, and productivity. Notice how, as a result of cross-training, your own players become all-stars and your staff a business Dream Team.

Fire Employees

Who Don't Meet Your Standards

In the 1997 Hollywood romantic comedy *My Best Friend's Wedding,* a scene opens with a maniacal master chef exploding at an assistant in the kitchen of a ritzy Chicago restaurant. "If you don't get this right," he thunders at his underling, "I'll kill your whole family!" The man playing the cameo role of chef in the movie was not an actor: he was Charlie Trotter.

While Trotter relished the film's parody of a "stereotypical screaming chef," he does understand the zeal for perfection that drives the character. Staff members understand it, too, and know that at Charlie Trotter's, they must adhere to a set of exceptional standards—or they're out the door.

Before going too much further, a word to the soft-hearted: once you've hired selectively and trained your staff to strive for excellence, it's unlikely you'll have to fire many employees. (What's more likely is that a number will quit after realizing they don't belong in a company that demands so much.) Nonetheless, you need to act firmly and swiftly when the situation dictates it.

Trotter's restaurant once hired a chef with excellent skills. The man preferred to operate solo, however, refusing to communicate in any way with teammates, even during the busiest Saturday night shifts. Though the chef's supervisor explained how his lack of teamwork was undermining the quality of the whole department—holding up completion of dishes at critical times during service—his attitude never improved. Eventually, though his culinary skills had proven excellent and his standards impeccable, he couldn't work as part of the team and had to be fired.

You may be someone who hates having to fire people. Perhaps you feel sorry for them, worrying about what they will do without a steady income and where they'll find another job. However, individuals who don't meet your standards and don't change after repeated warnings need to be sent packing. Remember that you're only as good as the weakest link in your chain. Without getting rid of dead weight, you'll never be able to create an excellent business.

Employers seeking to build a winning company need to protect themselves from wrongful discharge suits. To make sure you aren't taken to the cleaners, you'll want to take the following steps:

1. Provide employees with the company's disciplinary policies when they're hired and ask them to sign a form indicating that they've read the rules.
2. When individuals don't meet your standards, give verbal warnings, followed by written warnings (dangerous or criminal offenses such as drug use merit immediate termination).
3. Carefully document disciplinary meetings and annual performance reviews.
4. Act consistently when implementing disciplinary action.

To get started, you need to include a description of your company's policies in your employee handbook. Define your company's standards and what behavior is unacceptable in the workplace; the list will be relatively easy to compile. Record it in the company handbook, keeping it as short and simple as possible. Label a section "Employee Rights" and clearly spell out the progressive nature of the warning process and the documentation to which employees are entitled. (You'll also want to advise the staff to take verbal warnings seriously.) Next, specify the disciplinary outcomes associated with particular offenses or behaviors. Clearly, dangerous or criminal behaviors such as physical fighting, theft, drug use, sexual assault, and carrying a concealed weapon should always lead to immediate dismissal—not to mention police intervention. Other unacceptable types of behavior, while not criminal, can also be harmful to the company. Consider the following list of standards employed by Trotter's, then add your own:

Attendance: Individuals who call in sick every other week are probably not—more likely their absences stem from hangovers or late nights on the town. You don't have time to moonlight as a police investigator, so instead set a number of acceptable sick absences without a doctor's letter. Decide how many tardy arrivals are acceptable and make sure every employee knows the rules. Excellence requires strict discipline. Employees who report late to work could be sent home without pay.

Dress code: Appearance is no minor matter. You expect your staff to dress appropriately, so give them clear parameters. Require employees to wear clothing that is clean, pressed, and unstained, plus request they be clean-shaven and well groomed. For women, spell out whether or not they need to wear heels, stockings, and suits, and request they wear their hair up if necessary. For men, give guidelines regarding ties, suits, shirts, pants, shoes, facial hair, length of hair, and jewelry. More than three violations merit a written warning; repeated infractions should be grounds for discharge.

Meticulousness: Since you're reading this book, you undoubtedly value careful execution and focus. Explain to the staff that your company cannot tolerate repeated carelessness, sloppiness, and errors that result from lack of concentration. Ask yourself: Which errors are most serious? Which are a result of insufficient training? How many errors are unacceptable in a month? In the company handbook, cite examples of major infractions.

Professionalism and attitude: Employees need to understand they are expected to conduct themselves as mature, responsible adults. You can develop a list outlining unprofessional behavior: horsing around on the job, unsavory language, tantrums, and disrespect of customers or management. Where attitude is concerned, develop a list of behaviors such as sarcastic responses that will illicit warnings. Explain that three warnings, including a written warning, will lead to dismissal. Let employees know they need to be friendly, courteous, warm, upbeat, and enthusiastic at all times. Those who can't muster up a positive attitude will most likely have a demoralizing effect on coworkers and cannot be a productive member of your team.

Product knowledge: Those who don't appreciate your company's significant investment in training probably don't belong there. In the handbook, spell out the level of product knowledge you expect of your staff. State that those who fail written or oral exams more than two or three times a year will be looking for other work.

Time management: Employees who miss deadlines frequently should be penalized. In the handbook, specify your company's course of action. Each missed deadline should result in a verbal warning. More than three within a year should lead to a written warning and demotion or termination.

Before you move on, think of any additional standards and consider appropriate disciplinary actions. While you should *correct* offenders immediately and publicly for transgressions such as tardiness or disrespect, don't offer formal verbal warnings in front of the whole staff. When it's necessary to issue such warnings, meet with employees in a private area, such as your office.

How to Give a Warning

Even though you won't always hand individuals a written warning, it's a good idea to keep dated notes to which you can refer during a performance review. At such time, you should discuss the company policy or standard the employee violated; explain why it is so important he or she follow these rules; explain what the disciplinary action is or will be the next time; and determine what the person can do in the future to meet the standard. It's wise to conclude the meeting on a positive note and express your faith in the employee and his or her abilities.

Some situations will require you to issue a written warning for repeated offenses. The memo or letter must include the date, the employee's name, the manager's name, the standard that has not been met, the number of infractions, and the consequences if the behavior occurs again. No matter what, give the individual a copy and keep a copy for your records. If relations are especially acrimonious, be cautious and have the letter notarized.

REMEMBER THAT YOU'RE ONLY AS GOOD AS THE WEAKEST LINK IN YOUR CHAIN. WITHOUT GETTING RID OF DEAD WEIGHT, YOU'LL NEVER BE ABLE TO CREATE AN EXCELLENT BUSINESS.

As a matter of integrity, it's important to be considerate and fair to your staff—even those you're dismissing. Whatever you do, be consistent when it comes to disciplinary action (you don't want to fire one person for three unauthorized sick absences in one month and merely issue a warning to another). Employees who can establish they've been singled out and disciplined for actions that are common at your company will have a strong wrongful discharge case, particularly if coworkers can corroborate their stories. After you take these steps, you should be confident you have given employees every opportunity to change and you'll know you've done the right thing.

Time's Up

After you've exhausted every disciplinary measure and the time has come to fire someone, call the employee into your office and have all the relevant documentation at hand, including notes from verbal warnings, copies of the written warnings, and performance reviews. Respectfully tell the person that he or she is terminated, effective immediately, and explain exactly why, citing the standards that have not been met and the dates you issued warnings both verbally and in writing.

It's necessary to document the dismissal in much the same way you documented the written warning and to provide a copy for the employee. Of course, you need to include in the letter a statement to indicate you have discharged the individual for violations of company policies; specify which ones and the dates warnings were issued. To cushion the blow, give the person his last paycheck and offer fair severance pay, such as one to two weeks' salary for every year of service. (This is a policy you might *not* want to list in the handbook: it is a privilege, rather than an entitlement.)

Why some managers fire employees and then give them two to three weeks to "wrap things up" is an enigma. How could such an employee possibly be motivated to perform? After the meeting, it's safest to escort the employee back to his work area or locker and allow him to gather his belongings under your supervision. Occasionally, some disgruntled employees steal company files, materials, and documents, or simply trash the place in anger.

No matter what, don't let terminated employees change your mind. Though they might cry, scream, plead, or become belligerent, you need to be unwavering. Otherwise, the remaining employees won't take your standards seriously and they'll resent the fact that while they've been busy keeping up standards and discipline, some individuals have committed infractions and gotten away with them.

Excellence is sometimes tough. Get used to it.

your staff
(part ii):

EXCELLENCE IN

LEADERSHIP AND

MANAGEMENT

13 Set the Tone Every Day

"Actions speak louder than words," goes the old adage, and when it comes to setting the tone at your business, that saying is 100 percent accurate. To be a superb leader, you don't have to be sensationally charismatic—but you do need to act as a truly passionate and inspirational model for your staff all day, every day.

Why the dramatics? you might ask. Isn't the expectation of "a job well done" enough?

To achieve excellence, your company needs to do exceptional work on a regular basis. And passion allows employers and employees with ordinary skills and experience to do extraordinary things. Employees won't strive for excellence simply because they are told to. Someone needs to show them what it takes to deliver excellence, and that someone needs to be you.

At his Chicago restaurant, Charlie Trotter holds himself wholly responsible for creating an atmosphere of excellence. As his own toughest critic, Trotter is constantly and visibly striving to improve himself as a chef, a CEO, an artist, and a human being. In doing so, he sets the standard for the work environment at his restaurant— standards every staff member must meet. Comments psychiatrist and occasional Trotter's chef Dr. Howard Alt, "Trotter leads by example. You get on his juggernaut for as long as you want to be. Some people fall off, some people hang on."

Employees that stick it out recall absorbing Trotter's perfectionist standards almost through osmosis. Consider a typical afternoon at the restaurant: As usual, Trotter's management staff arrives at the restaurant early to begin preparations for the evening meal. They hang up their coats, adjust their suits and uniforms, then head for their stations. Greeting them even before they have a chance to think is a voicemail message from Chef Trotter, recorded at midnight from a hotel room in New Orleans—or New York, or Miami—where he's gone to give a lecture or present a cooking demonstration. Before leaving Chicago, Trotter's voice tells them, he noticed important oversights that need attention before customers arrive: "The wine bottles on the upper left-hand rack, third row from the left, are out of chronological order. Please see that they are reorganized according to the vintage year. Also, the cups next to the cappuccino machine are spotted. They will need to be rewashed and wiped. Over and out."

"When Trotter calls in and directs your attention to these kinds of nuances," says one floor manager, "you find yourself not only scrutinizing, say, the coffee cups, but the silverware in the drawer next door as well. Even more so when he's there. You'll be walking along, talking to Charlie in the restaurant, when all of a sudden, he'll stop in his tracks and straighten a picture. By doing so, he shows he's paying attention to every detail. As a result, you as an employee become more aware of your surroundings."

Aware that he's setting the tone for the entire operation, Trotter is passionate even when he's exhausted, and he's enthusiastic first thing in the morning and last thing at night. "Trotter's enthusiasm for what he does radiates throughout the organization," says Sara Lee COO Steve McMillan, a regular customer at the restaurant.

To achieve true excellence, it's essential your organization and your employees continuously improve. Who should be the first and most radical when it comes to self-improvement? You. Let your employees see you constantly devising ways to improve your work if you expect them to continuously improve theirs. To figure how to increase your level of passion and set the tone for excellence in your own business, you may need to go about it backwards—focusing on the aspects of your job you *hate,* not the parts you love. Identify times of day, responsibilities, tasks, or circumstances that incite very little interest in you. Then take action. Take a hard look at your own personal weaknesses, from the serious to the seemingly insignificant, and find real ways to strengthen them. Afraid of new technology? Find a trainer who can guide you through it during off-hours. Not a "morning person"? Go to bed earlier or skip your second margarita. Setbacks hard for you to take? Make a list of all the things for which you are grateful.

CHICAGO TRIBUNE COLUMNIST BILL RICE SEES A HINT OF THE RESPECTED MILITARY OFFICER IN TROTTER: "BECAUSE HE WORKS ALONGSIDE EMPLOYEES, THEY KNOW HE WON'T ASK THEM TO DO ANYTHING HE'S NOT WILLING TO DO HIMSELF. THEY ALSO KNOW HE WON'T SEND THEM ON MISSION: IMPOSSIBLE."

Remember: your mission is to lead by setting a stirring example. To do so, you'll need to grapple with the toughest questions: Do I work harder than anyone in the company? Am I willing to admit when I'm wrong? Do I pitch in and help people when they need help? Am I positive? Am I willing to do anything to deliver excellence? Can employees count on me to be there when they need me? Am I willing to accept change? Am I ever careless in my work?

Many young entrepreneurs have the idea that once their business is up and running, they'll hand over day-to-day operations to responsible and competent staff. Don't make this mistake and assume that your employees will know you're away taking care of important matters, or that they will understand you can't manage every aspect of the business. What they'll see is that you have priorities other than an excellent business. What seems obvious is sometimes forgotten: in this case, you can't lead by example when you're not there. First and foremost, you've got to show up to your business site. No exceptions, no excuses.

To convince them your demands and standards are reasonable, work side by side with your staff. *Chicago Tribune* columnist Bill Rice sees a hint of the respected military officer in Trotter: "Because he works alongside employees, they know he won't ask them to do anything he's not willing to do himself. They also know he won't send them on Mission: Impossible."

As a leader, you're faced with the age-old double duty: get the work done *and* keep morale high among the troops. One of the best ways to demonstrate dedication is to put forth a massive effort and work harder than anyone in your employ. With such an example, your employees will be more likely to give the job everything they've got, too. In the meantime, however, it's critical to be upbeat and optimistic, even if things aren't going as planned. Your entire staff is looking to you for encouragement and support. Even if you are tired, you can't let them know you are dragging. On the other hand, relentless diligence may be admirable, but it can turn the air to lead. It's also your responsibility to lighten up when the atmosphere gets too oppressive, so be positive and have fun when the situation calls for it.

Trotter knows that to command respect as a leader, you must not only talk values and standards, but also "walk the talk." Let staff see you do some of the grunt work—cleaning, answering phones, photocopying, and sending faxes. Observes software company CEO, international food and wine connoisseur, and longtime customer Steve Greystone, "Trotter gets the most out of his people and his staff because they know he will be there working on his day off, doing whatever it takes. Charlie doesn't say, 'I'm the boss, you guys do the work.' Instead, he's the first one to pitch in and do whatever it takes to get the job done. He doesn't care if he has gotten two hours' sleep—and his people see that. They know he's driven and he has only one thing in mind, and that's to make the restaurant the best it can be."

Create Anxiety

to Get the Most Out of Your Employees

In wartime, anxiety fills the air like a surging electric current. The besieged assume a state of readiness, and even the most conflictive society turns its energy toward becoming a tightly functioning unit. All citizens make their greatest effort for the common good; petty animosities are forgotten. Acts of individual heroism abound.

As a business owner, you've got a battle of your own, striving for excellence over mediocrity. Like a wartime general, you need to keep your employees on red alert at all times. While it's not a great idea to create a disablingly stressful atmosphere, it is your job to make sure no staff member lolls around in the comfort zone for long. You want your workers to expect and accept constant change, knowing full well that change induces fear in most humans. To be blunt, you want anxiety.

According to Charlie Trotter, the best motivational leaders create a tolerable level of "productive, playful anxiety" by constantly transforming workplace "constants." Trotter thrives in such an atmosphere, and he relishes formal events where anxiety is high. "Whenever people have to dress in black tie and attend a function where they might not know everybody, they're always a little bit on edge," says Trotter. "It keeps people on their toes intellectually and emotionally. Some of the most stimulating conversations result. People quickly become comfortable, but at first there is this heightened anxiety."

Your presence itself should cause hypervigilance in your employees. Even on days when mountains of paperwork or a slew of phone calls occupy you, pop out occasionally to inspect work, supervise staff members, and instruct people who are standing around chatting to get back to work. Make sure they know you'll be around at all times to keep them on their toes.

Charlie Trotter almost never misses a day at the restaurant. He makes sure he is at the restaurant or in the adjoining office over eighty hours a week. As a result, his staff is both perpetually on guard and extremely conscientious. Making his rounds, Trotter reminds his staff that customer expectations are tremendous because of the attention the restaurant has received locally, nationally, and abroad. For most of his staff, that constant reminder creates pressure and anxiety enough. After the restaurant receives favorable recognition, Trotter reminds his employees in no uncertain terms of the rare air they breathe. Employees had better rise to the occasion, Trotter tells them, because customers come to the restaurant with the expectation it will be the best meal they have ever had. One dining room manager recalls the effect of such a campaign at Trotter's. "The induction into the Relais and Chateaux was recognition we worked very hard for. And you know what? When we got it, our responsibility increased." The greater variety of responsibilities you give employees, the more anxious—and motivated—they'll be. You've completed cross-training; you can now expect employees to perform several different jobs almost simultaneously. If your business has not received formal recognition, you can reiterate customer praise and commendations to remind the staff of high expectations and the competition they are up against.

Trotter changes his menu every day, allowing no one to rest on the laurels of their previous successes. At Trotter's, "the constant innovation keeps them on their toes big time," says *Chicago Tribune* restaurant reviewer Phil Vettel. "Even with some of the trickiest plate presentations at other restaurants, after cooks have done their fiftieth one, they get pretty darned good at it. But cooks have no such luxury with Chef Trotter. He is going to have them do it one way and tomorrow it will be a different presentation." Concludes Vettel, "Being on staff at Trotter's must be the equivalent of being a soap-opera star. You walk in one morning and they say, 'Sorry, we have fifteen pages of script change' and they film in an hour."

Besides new product introductions and line extensions, you could also frequently introduce new equipment (whether machinery or computer software) and develop new techniques with employee input. Whatever the tactic, the goal is to keep employees guessing what will be dropped in their laps next.

Few assignments are more nerve-wracking for employees than public speaking. Another excellent way to reap the benefits of employee anxiety is to require them to speak in front of the entire company, whether to present their findings on a research project, offer their recommendations on how to improve the communication of information, or describe their plan to develop business in a sales territory. When they know a crowd is apt to be present, you can bet people will work much harder to get their facts straight and present a convincing argument.

There's nothing like a surprise attack to induce high-scale anxiety. Think back to high school and the pop-quiz assaults by your toughest science teacher. If you knew a given teacher had a penchant for unannounced tests, you prepared extra well for that class. That's why it makes sense to randomly shoot queries at your employees— and let them know you expect good answers. Out of the blue, ask them questions about product characteristics, origin, composition, and features. Propose hypothetical scenarios and ask what technique or resource they would use to complete the project. Inject trick questions from time to time to heighten the anxiety, and watch them squirm. The purpose? Ultimately, they'll perform better than ever before. These tests are meant to prepare employees for the potentially volatile face-to-face contact with the public, where even the best-rehearsed acts can break down in no time. In other words, the "anxiety" climate Trotter creates helps to replicate the reality of dealing with the consumer.

Each of us—no matter how outgoing or gregarious—is somewhat anxious when working with new faces in an unfamiliar environment. This anxiety is part of the reason Trotter sends employees to work in other restaurants around the country. Whenever possible, invite your charges to assist you on business trips. The trip alone can fill some people with apprehension. Having to do a sales pitch in another city in front of a board or committee of strangers might be just the kind of anxiety on which some of your employees would thrive. Send them out into the jungle. Once they've found their bearings, their confidence will sky-rocket and their abilities will have taken the great leap forward.

ACCORDING TO CHARLIE TROTTER, THE BEST MOTIVATIONAL LEADERS CREATE A TOLERABLE LEVEL OF "PRODUCTIVE, PLAYFUL ANXIETY" BY CONSTANTLY TRANSFORMING WORKPLACE "CONSTANTS." TROTTER THRIVES IN SUCH AN ATMOSPHERE, AND HE RELISHES FORMAL EVENTS WHERE ANXIETY IS HIGH.

Set Deadlines, Prioritize,

and React Quickly When Things Don't Get Done

Deadlines make the world go round. They allow office buildings to go up, retail store shelves to be stocked, and daily newspapers to be printed and delivered to your doorstep at dawn. Deadlines also make it possible for a high-powered chef-entrepreneur like Charlie Trotter to write several books, host a PBS televised cooking show, create retail products, consult for food-service companies, give interviews to journalists, and seat customers at 6 p.m., serving them an *amuse-gueule* shortly thereafter.

As an entrepreneur, deadlines are one of your best management tools. They allow you to supervise and motivate employees without having to physically or continuously monitor their work. Best of all, when you set deadlines—and consistently penalize employees who miss them—your staff members will eventually learn to manage themselves. Employees who want to loaf around during normal working hours will know they need to meet their deadlines by putting in long hours and working weekends or they won't last.

CEOs dining at Charlie Trotter's have witnessed just how tight a ship Trotter keeps and discover that, whether it's producing a fine pâté or a software package, Trotter's brand of strict adherence to timetables is what keeps a company buoyant. Says Steve Greystone, "Many times, at the office, I think of Charlie when I'm looking at the challenges of running our business and managing employees. I say, 'At Trotter's, they'd never get away with that type of attitude.' Coming in late for work, personal phone calls. Taking liberties that so many employees in so many businesses do. If Charlie were running the show, they'd be called on it. His employees know there's only one way to do things—the right way, or you just don't do them."

To prevent employees from setting loose deadlines for themselves, it's essential that you spell out exactly *what* you need and *when* you need it. First, identify the tone, style, content, thoroughness, detail, quantity, structure, and format specifications required for a specific job. Then set *exact* dates and times when you want the project or task finished. Never tell employees to perform an assignment "as soon as possible." What if the soonest he can see himself getting to it is next month? Indeed, superiors who give their charges such vague directives have no grounds to stand on when the work isn't done.

In your mind, your assignments and deadlines are probably crystal clear. That doesn't mean your employees see it the same way. For reasons ranging from fear of reprimand to simple carelessness to a skewed desire to "keep the peace," employees don't always speak up when they haven't understood what really needs to be done. To avoid these situations, review the deadlines with employees to be sure they understand what is required and expected of them, and ask them directly if they have any questions or concerns.

When Charlie Trotter contracts to write a book for his publisher, he breaks the work down into its most essential components and assigns deadlines to his staff and to himself. He assigns one cook to test 10 recipes a week, for example, instead of dumping into someone's lap an impossible 100 recipes in ten weeks.

So that there's no doubt about your deadlines, put them in writing. That way, if work isn't done on time, you've documented the order and are entitled to carry out disciplinary action. For regularly scheduled tasks, ask managers and supervisors to provide a day-by-day or weekly "to-do" list for each of their charges. For those occasions when you're out of the office or away from your desk and are calling in new instructions, leave yourself a voicemail message or write a note to remind yourself you gave them assignments.

How many hours, days, or weeks will it take to perform the

assigned tasks? Knowing this will allow you to set reasonable deadlines. Take, for example, your company newsletter. The writer needs one week to compose it, the editor three days to hone the writing. Your graphic artist will need at least two days to design it, and the print shop a week to put it through the press. Therefore, you'll be making assignments on specific days and with very tight deadlines.

To determine how long tasks take to complete, managers must closely supervise the work—and to be absolutely sure, might perform the work themselves. Record how long it takes several employees to do the same job, then compute the average time it takes to perform tasks.

BEST OF ALL, WHEN YOU SET DEADLINES—AND CONSISTENTLY PENALIZE EMPLOYEES WHO MISS THEM—YOUR STAFF MEMBERS WILL EVENTUALLY LEARN TO MANAGE THEMSELVES.

When it comes to setting deadlines, turn the screws. After you figure out the average length of time it takes to execute a task or assignment, subtract a few hours or days and set tight deadlines. Charlie Trotter knows through personal experience that with focus, drive, and dedication, an assignment that takes five days to complete can be completed in four or less. After employees are able to comfortably meet your tight deadlines, make them even tighter. Employees will become increasingly efficient and be able to handle increased workloads. But don't set impossible goals. When employees are never able to meet deadlines, they begin to regard the deadlines as goals to shoot for rather than actual due dates. Motivation and drive to meet the deadline wanes, defeating the purpose of the entire process. Striking the balance is a skill you'll hone over time.

Keep the energy current by setting deadlines only weeks or days in advance. Say you intend to open a new outlet in the future, and you know you're going to need to begin a business plan for it in a year. There's really no point in asking employees to think about work so far in the future. They're likely to forget the deadline, and if anything, it will distract them from the work at hand.

Setting Priorities: When First Comes First

On rare occasions, project deadlines may need to be delayed to accomplish an unforeseen but absolutely essential task. For example, say you've assigned your administrative assistant the task of fine-tuning the employee handbook. Suddenly, out of the blue, you are awarded a lucrative production contract that requires immediate start-up. Or perhaps your biggest client has called to say she's stopping by your office, and the place needs to be spotless. Under such circumstances, the company handbook will have to be put on hold while your assistant tackles the more immediate, client-related work.

Prioritizing, the tricky task of ranking your company's various functions and projects in order of importance, comes down to a matter of trade-offs. As company head, you've got to know your own priorities in advance. Like Charlie Trotter's, your company's first priority should be to provide superior-quality products, service, and value. Trotter would never compromise his commitment to excellence by prioritizing a short-term opportunity over his big-picture values. Forced to make a choice between, say, giving a press interview or being on hand at the restaurant when a crisis occurs, the restaurant prevails every time.

Your staff members often have complex job descriptions. They might answer to a range of managers, requiring completion of several tasks at once. As such, they'll need training in how to rank their responsibilities in order of importance. Especially during his first months on the job, have your new hire write up a priorities list, which you or a manager then evaluates. After going through this exercise week after week, you'll feel increasingly confident about allowing him to make decisions independently. Until that time, don't assume he'll intuitively know the right course of action.

Dealing with Missed Deadlines

You've explained to employees how important it is to the company's quest for excellence that they perform their work on time. When they don't, you must react immediately and firmly. If an employee misses a deadline, you might begin by eliminating certain perks that are part of his employment package.

On those rare occasions when a deadline cannot be met for legitimate reasons, ask employees to warn you in advance. In cases of good judgment, reward employees for advising you by not penalizing them as severely as those who sweep unfinished work under the rug. Next, determine if they're able to finish the work by putting forth greater effort, or if they need assistance.

A worker who routinely misses deadlines despite warnings should be dismissed. That's the surest way to show how serious you are about getting work done on time.

Precise Directions

Lead to Precise Results

Like a master jeweler, your excellent business can't afford imprecise results. You count on your employees to work precisely to your specifications. Whether you're a chef, sports coach, contractor, retailer, or magazine editor, you'll need to direct your team with very clear and easily understood language.

To issue assignments effectively, you'll need to begin by asking yourself a variety of questions. You'll consider:

- Measurements (weight, temperature, dimensions, speed, quantity)

- Style (tone, quality, character, form, type, color, flavor, convention)

- Content (components, ingredients, topics, physical detail, facts, information)

- Methods (processes, procedures, techniques)

- Features (special attributes, characteristics)

- Format (shape, arrangement, construction, order, organization).

A contractor managing a team of house painters might first look at dimension, the size of the job, and then its characteristics, considering many different questions: What's the size of the overall area to cover? What color will the walls be? What type and brand of paint should be used? What type of prep work is necessary? How much time should the team spend painting each room? What kind of special effects would enliven the space? Is there a particular method the team should use? Do the rooms need to be painted in a particular order?

Chef Trotter realizes that precise results are absolutely vital to the pursuit of excellence. At his restaurant, the menu, featuring twenty-five or more dishes, evolves continuously. Imagine the daunting challenge faced by the kitchen staff each day as they work behind the scenes, cutting, shaping, seasoning, cooking, garnishing, and serving—all to the chef's precise specifications.

In many businesses, there is little or no room for employee interpretation (or misinterpretation). In restaurants, for example, glassware is always placed at the top and to the right of dinner plates; bread plates are always to the left. Salad, appetizer, and dinner forks are positioned on the left side, knives and spoons to the right.

On the other hand, many kinds of assignments require creativity. In your business, determine if a certain task allows for creativity by asking yourself if there is just one right way to perform the task. If you can think of more than one way, then it means creativity plays a part in the outcome. Charlie Trotter sometimes allows his staff to choose an ingredient they want to prepare on a particular evening and he largely develops the dish. Occasionally, Trotter chooses the ingredients he wants a cook to use and allows him to decide how they should be prepared. Senior kitchen staff such as Chef de Cuisine Matthias Merges are allowed more input and often create from scratch.

Which part and how much of the creative process will you entrust to employees and which part will you reserve for yourself? Once you're sure, start thinking about precise ways to convey the information. You've determined measurements, style, content, methods, features, and format; now you need to communicate these specifics to your staff.

Let's say you're a juice bar owner in a busy urban center. Your business offers the harried office crowd a much-needed infusion of fresh fruit and vegetables—from peaches to papaya, wheatgrass to beets. You hire a new employee; you're giving her instructions from scratch. Remember, think *precise*. Don't ask her to use "a lot of berries" in each raspberry smoothie she serves. Instead, explain what you need in cups or ounces. Specify set amounts of vanilla bean and powdered sugar she'll use, rather than simply saying you want the drinks to be "sweet." Specify the style of glass to use and the temperature at which it should properly be served.

Charlie Trotter's precise instructions to employees more closely resemble those of a diamond cutter than a typical culinary entrepreneur. With the chef, it's not enough to say he wants carrots cut. He specifies finely chopped, chopped, sliced, finely diced, diced, julienned, or finely julienned. Terms or phrases specific to your own industry can be a great asset, as long as your employees genuinely understand what each term means. Don't just assume they do. Instead, assure new hires that when they don't understand jargon, it's perfectly fine, and even required, that they ask for a definition.

On occasions when it's simply too difficult or time-consuming to communicate what you require in words, explain what you want by showing employees. A house painter might demonstrate a brush stroke to a trainee rather than try to spell out the amount of paint used, the position of the hand, the speed and force of the stroke.

Let's face it: both you and your employees might forget exactly what the assignment is if it's not written. To ensure work is done exactly how you want it to be done, take the time to type work assignments. That way, employees have guidelines to which they can refer as many times as needed, and they cannot easily argue when they fail to follow your directions. Plus, you will be better able to review their work to ensure it was completed to your exact specifications.

For tasks that are too simple to merit a typed description, train employees to take notes whenever you ask them to do odds and ends. When Trotter wishes a waiter to offer a customer a dessert course not listed on the menu, he's certainly not going to run to the office to type a memo about it, but he does expect his server to make a note of the request so she won't forget.

TROTTER'S PRECISE INSTRUCTIONS TO EMPLOYEES MORE CLOSELY RESEMBLE THOSE OF A DIAMOND CUTTER THAN A TYPICAL CULINARY ENTREPRENEUR.

A recipe not only requires that ingredients be cut, measured, and prepared in certain ways, but also directs the cook to prepare the dish in a particular order. Your employees need the same clear, spelled-out order. You can't present a company report before earnings figures have been compiled anymore than you can sauté a whole onion and then peel and finely dice it. Your new employee might not know that. To make sure you're recording the steps correctly, perform the assignment yourself at least once or observe an experienced employee.

No matter how clear and concise you attempt to be in your assignments, invariably employees will not understand certain points, either because you haven't communicated to them well enough or because they lack the knowledge or expertise. That's why you need to go over work assignments with your staff to make sure they understand what you want. Be proactive and ask them questions regarding the material. Ask: Do you have any questions? Do you understand everything? Do you understand what I mean when I ask for a squab roasted medium-rare? Then explain or demonstrate what you need. Keep it simple, but above all, keep it precise.

17 Take Responsibility
for the Details

Star Wars director and special-effects genius George Lucas is a sound fanatic. Passionate from childhood days about all things cinematic, Lucas determined as an adult to make the finest theater sound system in existence for moviegoers. Today, before any theater opens with his cutting-edge THX sound system, Lucas visits the place personally, pacing the aisles from entrance to screenside, making sure that the system has been installed and acoustics are impeccable. If a theater doesn't meet his standards, Lucas won't authorize use of the THX system—even if it means that his own *Star Wars* prequels, which can be shown only in THX, cannot be seen.

This lesson is about taking responsibility for the details. To do so, you and your staff must identify all the detail-oriented elements of your business and work like crazy to attend to each one. Your primary job as a leader and manager is to never compromise. To attend to all the details of your business requires a tremendous investment of time and energy, but a business that takes responsibility for them is destined for excellence.

Charlie Trotter has been haunted by a seemingly insurmountable problem. Lint balls. Yes, lint balls. To him, the pesky lint balls seem to have a life of their own, gravitating almost purposely onto the restaurant's fine dining-room carpets. Because Trotter finds them unsightly, and because it's impossible to vacuum when guests are seated, lint balls were one of his pet peeves—one he wouldn't give up on solving.

Recently, after Trotter spent yet another period pondering this irritating detail, he had an idea: he could develop double-sided adhesive strips that employees would stick to the bottoms of their shoes to allow them to discreetly pick up lint, debris, and crumbs on the dining room floor, return to a station, peel the adhesive off, and throw it away. Some readers might say to themselves, "All that for lint balls? This guy must be nuts." In Trotter's mind, the lint balls reflect poorly on his establishment, and he'll do anything to remove them without disturbing his guests.

Though it's important for you as a leader to envision the future and look at the "big picture," you can't be above the details. As a matter of fact, you have to demonstrate to employees what it means to attend to the details. You have to take the time to do everything the right way, constantly spot details that are overlooked, meticulously review your staff's work, carefully execute your own work, and scrupulously clean and organize, because remember—you set the tone.

For Charlie Trotter, every aspect of the business, from the grand to the minuscule, merits the utmost attention to detail. The chef's own appearance is no exception. Daily, the chef arrives neatly groomed and impeccably dressed. Crumbs on the floor, artwork hanging crooked, or smudges on the stemware rarely escape his notice. In the kitchen, he reviews everyone's work methodically, "leaving no truffle unturned."

Employees can learn the importance of attention to detail in both conscious and subconscious ways. In addition to purchasing high-quality raw materials, don't be afraid to spend money on decorating, fine furnishings, artwork, lighting, flowers, and plants, especially in retail businesses. At Trotter's, the wall covering is a very expensive custom-woven, one-of-a-kind fabric that was specially backed like wallpaper, then Scotchguarded and hung. Many customers don't realize it's unique, but Trotter knows they would surely be "underwhelmed" if the restaurant hung ordinary commercial-grade paper. Similarly, the beautifully upholstered chairs feature handmade, all-natural fabrics. Not only are these peerless pieces expensive to manufacture, but they are also very costly to maintain.

Even with these investments, your greatest challenge will be to convince employees that the details collectively constitute the masterpiece: your excellent business. One of the best ways to do that is to talk about attention to detail all the time. It's smart to share with employees examples of details that are missed or ignored in other businesses and use them as teaching tools. You won't have much trouble finding examples. With today's self-service, no-frills, hyper-casual business atmosphere, customer service standards careen toward mediocrity—or worse.

It's important to note that your standards must be immutable. One longtime Trotter's customer was dining at the restaurant on Valentine's Day, a very busy evening. Owing to the many glasses of water and several glasses of wine she enjoyed, the customer had to visit the rest room on several occasions. Each and every time, a service person escorted her to the rest room, opened the door, checked to be sure it was spotless, and ensured the towels and toilet paper were stocked and neatly arranged. Busy or not, it's the service staff's job to make sure these details aren't overlooked.

A great way to convince your staff that all the details collectively make the difference between excellence and mediocrity is to think up memorable "transformation" fantasies from real-life examples. Pick a business or industry that is known for poor service or products, and then imagine what it would be like if they attended to the details. Share the image with your employees.

Because so many of his staff arrive to and from work in Chicago taxis, Trotter likes to invent such a "transformation" scenario for one of the city's most notoriously slipshod taxi cartels. In a detail-oriented world, the outfit's taxis are spotless inside and out, they're comfortable, and they have no unpleasant odors. Courteous, well-mannered taxi drivers offer customers a folded copy of a local newspaper, and inquire if they would prefer to listen to a particular radio station and if they have a preferred route. If drivers only attended to a few details, prompts Trotter, the taxi odyssey could be turned into a refined and pleasurable excursion.

There are thousands of details in any business. Your job is to identify every detail involved in the daily running of your business and, when possible, set standards for each one. Think about every nook and cranny in your facility and set standards of cleanliness, tidiness, order, organization, and appearance. Chairs, tables, and product displays need to be aligned, shelves stocked, carpets cleaned regularly, countertops relieved of clutter and constantly wiped clean, rest room supplies stocked neatly, artwork hung straight, and files put in order.

You also need to search out details when it comes to products, packaging, marketing materials, and other documents. Goods must be packed impeccably. No matter what kind of business you're in, every document your company produces needs to be edited for style, grammar, and spelling, typeset on a word processor, and printed on a quality printer. For a personal touch, correspondence might be hand-addressed and stamped rather than labeled and metered. The sky's the limit when it comes to details.

To consistently attend to the details as an organization, there has to be strong supervision. Even though you set specific standards, employees will not always go the extra mile unless they know they're being watched. It's your job to spot deviations from your standards and examples of inattention to detail and point them out to employees immediately. You and your managers need to manage by walking around: spot-check to make sure products are wrapped or packaged neatly, facilities are spotless, and phones are answered promptly.

So you don't inadvertently overlook anything, create checklists and systems to help you to manage the details. Using checklists, you and your managers can easily inspect processes, such as cleaning the storeroom, stocking display units, and packaging perishable or fragile items. Provide written guidelines to illustrate how documents should be designed or written and how products should be assembled. At Charlie Trotter's, to guarantee no one waits too long for a course or is served consecutive courses without a reasonable intermission, each ticket used to place an order in the kitchen includes the time the guests are seated and the time each course is served.

TO ATTEND TO ALL THE DE-TAILS OF YOUR BUSINESS RE-QUIRES A TREMENDOUS IN-VESTMENT OF TIME AND ENERGY, BUT A BUSINESS THAT TAKES RESPONSIBILITY FOR THEM IS DESTINED FOR EXCELLENCE.

Above all, find a way to attend to details without inconveniencing guests. Intrusion in the name of attention to detail is like ducking under water in a rainstorm to keep from getting wet. Although you may want the carpets to be cleaned to impress customers with a ship-shape hotel lobby, for example, it's not smart to vacuum around customers' feet. Instead, train your employees to discreetly bend over and pick up garbage by hand. In retail businesses, instruct employees not to interrupt customers, linger too long in their personal space, or do anything that will disturb them.

your staff
(part iii):

THE ENTREPRENEUR

AS MOTIVATOR

Create Challenges for Your Employees

and Encourage Them to Challenge Themselves

For the many centuries up until the arrival of the Europeans, the Wampanog Indians of present-day Massachusetts partook in an uncompromising coming-of-age rite during the course of which young boys became adult members of the tribe. At the beginning of autumn, with only the simplest weapons and coverings, each boy was sent out alone into the forest for months. Winter would test the limits of his wits, resourcefulness, and stamina, revealing how well he had excelled at hunting, foraging, and survival skills he'd learned during his earliest years. While extreme by today's standards, this rigorous challenge allowed initiates to return with a profound sense of self-confidence and a clear vision of their abilities to contribute to the group.

The desire to be challenged is a powerful human motivation. If you're smart, you'll use it to get the most out of your employees—no matter how well established your company is. For while it's crucial to challenge staff in new and growing businesses, it's just as essential to stimulate employees in mature, nationally recognized firms.

For starters, you need to figure out what challenges your employees most. Don't assume everyone's motivated equally by the same kind of work, goals, deadlines, tests, or problems to be solved. One employee might find the task of drafting a company charter compelling; for another, meeting impossible deadlines gets his juices going. You may have in your midst a would-be sleuth who's thrilled by the challenge of tracking down lost records. An ultra-meticulous employee might find detective work a bore, but would jump at the chance to design a beautifully efficient archival database.

Take the time to observe who among your staff is unhappy, has too much time on their hands, or seems bored or apathetic. These signs point to insufficient challenges. In an interview session or in a short, written questionnaire, ask your staff the questions that will divulge what challenges will excite them most: Do you sometimes feel bored? When? Under what circumstances? What work do you find to be most difficult? What work makes you the most excited? What kind of goals do you consider to be most difficult to reach? How do you feel about change? Which jobs in the company do you want to learn? Can you handle more work? Do you believe you're sufficiently challenged? Do you have any trouble reaching your goals?

Once you've identified employees who need to be challenged more intensely, "turn the screws" by altering their set tasks or deadlines. "What's needed is such a big commitment that when people see what the goal will take, there's almost an audible gulp," say management educators James C. Collins and Jerry Porras in the *Harvard Business Review* (Sept/Oct, 1996).

For those who typically have no trouble meeting quotas, set very high sales goals. Ask employees who are great technicians but consider themselves poor salespeople to get on the phone and sell. Give additional projects to those who always have their work done ahead of schedule. Employees who have great difficulty handling several jobs simultaneously should be given several jobs simultaneously. You get the picture.

In the meantime, demand that your staff learn new industry-related information constantly. Just when they're beginning to think they know it all, give them additional books and materials to study, methods to hone, product features to memorize, computer programs to master, languages to learn, manual skills to develop, and contacts to pin down. As soon as employees reach a comfort level, give them something new to keep them on their toes. Then test them to make sure they're on board. It's important to set hard-to-reach performance goals not only for the group, but for individuals as well, particularly if your staff members have diverse responsibilities. Precise, visible targets will motivate individual employees and help raise your company's overall performance. Challenge employees to submit entries for individual industry awards for creativity and performance, or methods and products they invent and perfect. Like Charlie Trotter's sommeliers, or wine stewards (who, with Trotter's encouragement, entered international wine competitions and won), the challenge only drove them to new heights of expertise, at the same time greatly enhancing the prestige of the restaurant.

To be a truly motivational leader, stay a step ahead of your employees' needs, challenging them *before* they become bored or apathetic. Carefully observe employees, and ask them regularly how they feel about their work. Have promoted employees describe which parts of their former job they found unchallenging. At what point did they start to become bored or dissatisfied? If, because of declining sales projections or expiring customer contracts, you anticipate that your staff will have less work in the near future, advise employees in advance, rather than waiting until they're bored out of their minds. Prepare special projects to work on or bring in work from another department, even if it means additional training.

THE DESIRE TO BE CHALLENGED IS A POWERFUL HUMAN MOTIVATION. IF YOU'RE SMART, YOU'LL USE IT TO GET THE MOST OUT OF YOUR EMPLOYEES—NO MATTER HOW WELL ESTABLISHED YOUR COMPANY IS.

Be a Cheerleader

and Recognize Employees

We all yearn for approval and praise from our superiors, particularly when they're individuals we respect. As an effective leader, you need to positively reinforce excellent staff performance, so spur on your staff daily with applause and emotional exclamations of fighting spirit.

Skilled, effective leaders like Charlie Trotter motivate their troops by keeping them pumped up all the time. By encouraging his employees to take no shortcuts that might undermine integrity or product and service quality, Chef Trotter reminds them they have what it takes. During a dinner shift in full swing, Trotter is urging, prodding, praising, and pushing nonstop; the extent of his repertoire is notorious, featuring cheers for every challenge.

Stepping behind the scenes at Trotter's, a visitor would be treated to a verbal barrage coming from the boss's direction. "Come on—we really have to focus now," Trotter shouts. It's ten o'clock at night and he senses that his posse of chefs, exhausted after producing for an impromptu banquet of sixty-three airline executives, may be fading. "Keep focused—the next five minutes will be the key to the evening!" Trotter declares—then changes momentarily to a softer tact: "Sometimes we need to take the long, hard road, guys," he cajoles, as his assistants slice away at a side of lamb or prepare mounds of pepper and eggplant strips. "Keep your eyes on the prize. You know how much I hate the word compromise." Around 10:30 p.m., it's time for course number eight, but Trotter never lets up. "It's got to be perfect every time, team. One hundred percent effort every time. Concentrate. I said, *concentrate*. Customers expect us to deliver the same level of excellence every day. God is in the details. Let's make it the best experience they have ever had." At the dessert station in the kitchen, a new pastry chef is doing her darnedest to land a ball of ice cream atop warm, triangular fig turnovers, but the frozen scoops keep sliding off. Trotter sees she's close to a solution: "Stick with it, you're doing great," he interjects. Then he screams over her shoulder, "Let's see some energy, people. Help your teammate! What do they need? Figure it out!" With Trotter cheering them on, they nearly always do.

Beyond Cheerleading

Besides cheerleading, it's also your job to applaud employees when they exceed your expectations. Let your pacesetters know they're appreciated. Remind them how important their work is, being sure to give the credit they deserve for the company's success.

Few experiences are more motivational for staff members than being recognized for a fine performance individually, in front of one's peers. That's why it's a great idea for you to formally acknowledge an employee of the month, or at least, during staff meetings, to personally congratulate a staff member whose contributions to the company have gone beyond the call of duty. Let the individual know how important she is to the business and how her hard work sets an example for everyone. For the benefit of the group, spell out exactly why the individual is being recognized. That way, other employees will be motivated to receive your recognition in the future.

Praise should not, however, come cheap. As Charlie Trotter emphasizes, your commendations need to be genuine. As you might imagine, Trotter usually thinks he and his staff could do a better job. In his exacting mind, the restaurant and its staff always have "a long way to go" and much to achieve and accomplish. So while Trotter holds his employees and their hard work in exceptionally high esteem, he commends them only occasionally and selectively. Consequently, when he does acknowledge the staff or individuals for their work, it has a greater impact. They know they've really done something special.

When your entire company team is working hard and performing well together, give recognition to the whole group. Trotter often acknowledges everyone during the daily staff meeting. On particularly special occasions, he may go so far as to make a public spectacle of his praise, as he did at a recent high-profile Chicago culinary extravaganza. That afternoon, as is customary in their trade, Charlie Trotter's kitchen staff stayed largely behind the scenes. As the meal came to its satisfying conclusion, however, Trotter emerged from the kitchen with a twenty-strong brigade of cooks and assistants, every one of whom he introduced individually to the audience. "That just knocked over the people in the audience— that Trotter was that knowledgeable and concerned about his staff members, and willing to take the time to do that," says food and wine columnist Bill Rice of the *Chicago Tribune.* Even better, the cooks themselves were elated, returning to Trotter's kitchen more motivated than ever before.

"STICK WITH IT, YOU'RE DOING GREAT," [TROTTER] INTERJECTS. THEN HE SCREAMS OVER HER SHOULDER, "LET'S SEE SOME ENERGY, PEOPLE. HELP YOUR TEAMMATE! WHAT DO THEY NEED? FIGURE IT OUT!" WITH TROTTER CHEERING THEM ON, THEY NEARLY ALWAYS DO.

When your business is fortunate to be recognized with awards or in positive newspaper and magazine articles, share the acknowledgment with employees. Charlie Trotter's, for example, frequently earns award nominations and celebratory reviews from the media. The nominations for the James Beard Foundation Outstanding Service Award in 1995, 1996, 1997, 1998, and

1999 provided the staff with a much-coveted marker of acknowledgment for their hard work. Indeed, as Trotter often assures his troops, being nominated for an award is nearly as good as winning. The James Beard Awards are the Oscars of the culinary world, and Trotter reminds his staff what an honor it is to be considered among the top five service restaurants in the country. Make sure you share acknowledgment and joy with the people who helped to make it possible. Above all, no matter how tough the competition gets, keep that spirit high.

20 Give All Employees the Freedom to Reach the Top

A motivated employee is an employee who's confident that if she works hard and well, she's as likely to reach the top as the coworker next to her—regardless of gender, race, or other factors external to her performance. Indeed, one of the greatest motivators is to provide *all* your employees unlimited growth opportunities.

Before continuing, let's make something perfectly clear: we're not talking here about quotas or preferences—just simple logic. Your employees are your firm's greatest resource, and they always will be. Hindering select employees based on one's own personal prejudice or whims is a careless waste of a company's potential. By encouraging every employee to do their personal best and allowing them every opportunity to achieve top positions, you're adding solid value to your resource base.

Most employers don't deliberately set out to discriminate against their staff members on the basis of race, gender, or beliefs.

But the fact is, we're human—a rather narcissistic species—and as such, we frankly tend to promote people who most resemble ourselves. The dangers of discrimination lawsuits notwithstanding, solely advancing people just like us is bad for business and is bad business.

The idea of diversifying your employee base must go beyond the simplistic goal of "increasing the number of affinity groups on the payroll," write Harvard Business School's David A. Thomas and Columbia University's Robin J. Ely (*Harvard Business Review*, Sept/Oct 1996). Instead, diversity means "the varied perspectives and approaches to work that members of different identity groups bring." You want to have a staff that can offer varied and valuable insights into new trends and markets, as well as give important new ideas on how to reach goals, communicate, create teams more effectively, and conceptualize tasks. In other words, you want people with the information your company needs to remain both exceptional and competitive in a global economy. Overlooking the knowledge, skills, and potential of talented employees equals substantial losses to your public and business.

Take a good look at the demographic composition of your management team—not only with regard to upper management, but also lower and middle management. What percentage are women? What percentage are men? What percentage are Hispanic? White? Black? Asian? What percentage are in their twenties? Forties? Sixties? What percentage are college-educated? What percentage are single? Or married?

Observe other characteristics, such as appearance, political allegiance, areas of interests, and religion. Are most of your managers conventionally good-looking? Are they slim? Are they mainly liberal or conservative? Are they culture fanatics? Fitness nuts? Are they mostly Catholics, Evangelical Christians, Jews, Scientologists, Muslims? Most important, do your managers share most of these characteristics with you? If so, it may be a clear sign you don't give all employees the freedom to reach the top or that you have a hiring bias. You needn't promote people because they're different from you, but you'll do your business a favor by giving everyone an equal shake.

Devising an Opportunity-Rich Environment for All

Even if your employees are well-trained and determined, they can't be promoted if there aren't advanced positions available for them. The average business has a fair number of dead-end jobs, and such jobs can kill employee ambition and motivation. It's the mark of an excellent business when a company develops innovative ways to reward employee ambition.

"I'VE VERY RARELY BROUGHT ANYONE IN FROM THE OUTSIDE. I'VE ALWAYS BROUGHT PEOPLE UP, TRAINED THEM EXACTLY THE WAY I WANT TO TRAIN THEM. AS A RESULT, THEY HELP ME TO EXECUTE THE VISION THEY'VE LEARNED."

— Charlie Trotter

To truly provide opportunities for all employees, it's necessary to really do your homework and be creative. Start from the top: devise a range of new projects and consulting tasks to provide your employees with growth opportunities. Incorporate them into all aspects of your company—both in and away from headquarters. As Trotter's has expanded beyond the restaurant itself—providing consultation to a variety of corporations, publishing books, creating retail products, and catering private functions—a great range of new job and promotional opportunities have been created. For example, as his business transforms, Trotter has set Controller Judi Carle to work as book editor, restaurant manager Mark Signorio to work as architect and designer, and Chef de Cuisine Matthias Merges to work as company illustrator.

If you want to provide unlimited opportunities for your employees, don't hire managers from other companies. A strict promote-from-within policy sends employees a clear message that your company is serious about employee growth. Such a policy also helps ensure that your business will have a greater number of senior positions potentially available to whet the appetite of hard-working and enthusiastic employees who show promise.

It's also smart to provide lateral promotions. In restaurants, for example, there are few growth opportunities for busboys or dishwashers aside from supervisory positions in these departments, but high-performing busboys might be promoted to server or to cook. Employees with so-called "blue-collar" skills can be groomed for promotion if they possess fundamental strengths, like solid communication and organizational skills.

Remember also that because they have been indoctrinated and trained according to your standards, in-house staff members promoted to senior positions make better managers. Charlie Trotter takes full advantage of this strategy. "I've very rarely brought anyone in from the outside," he explains. "I've always brought people up, trained them exactly the way I want to train them. As a result, they help me to execute the vision they've learned."

Your basic rule of thumb in choosing whom to promote? Be consciously open-minded. Ask yourself questions that will yield objective answers: Does the candidate clearly desire the promotion? Has the employee asked about opportunities frequently? Has he or she expressed an interest in learning new skills or training others? Does the individual have a positive attitude? Is he or she willing to do anything to work up the ladder? Does the individual adapt easily to change? How do promotion candidates get along with their peers? Do they demonstrate solid communication or organizational skills?

Do they share the company's values and believe strongly in its vision?

Every six months, sit down with your employees as part of a review process and set goals through which they can attain the next level of skill or expertise. Perhaps a clerk with management potential needs to improve his written or oral communication skills before you'll feel comfortable promoting him to floor supervisor. Work with him to develop a strategy for reaching these career goals, say, by taking a class at a local university. Similarly, English courses might help foreign-born workers to excel.

Another way to groom employees for growth opportunities is to oversee training yourself. Perhaps a data entry worker needs to improve her overall organizational skills before she is ready to manage a complex database. Provide a mentor for her so that she can develop better systems for organization and effective "to-do" lists.

Finally, don't outsource work unless you absolutely have to. If your company must outsource particular projects—say, graphic design, management information services, or public relations work—consider giving your own talented employees an opportunity to work together with your consultants, overseeing and developing these projects. When you offer your own people the freedom to fly high, they'll bring your company up with them.

Allow Employees to
Do Work They Enjoy

Some employees want to be involved in *everything.* One of these worker-bee types may offer to help write marketing proposals, though she's managing accounts payable. Another may want to redesign the company Web page or redo the office interior, even though his expertise lies in public relations. As long as your employees complete their other responsibilities, Trotter says, don't discourage this type of behavior. Your job is to help them to figure out exactly what their skills are and what they want to do, then turn them loose to do work they enjoy.

Finding out what they enjoy can sometimes mean surprises, as Trotter himself found out during a recent publishing venture.

Trotter considers his cookbooks an important part of his restaurant's epicurean mission. His volumes sell widely and, in a very real sense, bring Charlie Trotter's exceptional cuisine into the kitchens of homes throughout the United States and Europe. Every element of the cookbooks—from recipes to text to graphic design—are key to the company image.

Last winter, Controller and cookbook editor Judi Carle sat doggedly searching for an illustrator whose renderings would match Trotter's vision. Artists from New York to Los Angeles submitted portfolios, and samples covered Carle's desk. Still, none seemed just right.

One evening Chef de Cuisine Matthias Merges passed by Carle's desk on his way to the kitchen. Glancing down at the mountain of artist's renderings, Merges scoffed, "Those people don't know food! You need an illustrator who knows food. I could do better than that!" At first, Carle thought Merges was simply criticizing—and jokingly challenged him to show his stuff. The next day Merges brought his sketchbook, which was filled with expert food illustrations ranging from rainbow trout and shiitake mushrooms to lipstick peppers and teardrop tomatoes. The staff loved the chef's drawings, and from that day on, Merges took on the additional responsibilities as resident illustrator.

Occasionally, employees will have skills that at first don't seem to have any application. With loyal, hard-working individuals, it's a good idea to create positions for them. Doing so pays off, often when you least expect it.

Mark Signorio, originally schooled in design, started at Charlie Trotter's as a waiter. Over the course of years, Signorio moved up the restaurant's ranks to general manager. His design experience seemed largely irrelevant to the needs of the gourmet restaurant and were all but forgotten. In 1995, however, Signorio's training was finally put to use.

That year, Trotter decided to add an addition to the establishment's second floor and had hired an architect to draw up plans. Management reviewed them. Signorio believed that the architect's vision was awkward and out-of-sync with Charlie Trotter's vision. To propose an alternative, the young service manager drew up some sketches. Roundly impressed, Trotter asked him to take over the project. Today, Signorio is the restaurant's staff designer, and director of marketing as well.

At Trotter's, scenarios like Signorio's have become general policy. Employees start with a basic job description—say, waiter, pantry chef, or host. Once they've become effective and efficient, the chef-owner allows them go in the direction they want to go. The result is a staff that's pleased and motivated. They're good at the work, doing what they enjoy and putting their skills to use. What's more, they see their own personal ingenuity making a difference.

Trotter later tapped Signorio to spearhead a number of major design and redesign projects. Among his many accomplishments, the designer has refurbished most elements of the restaurant (from the chairs and tables to the walls, floors, and carpets), designed a state-of-the-art wine cellar, enhanced the building's façade, and joined it with the restaurant's offices located in a town house next door. In contrast to the national trend toward increasingly rapid employee turnover, staff members like Signorio have remained with the company for over a decade. If they hadn't been encouraged to put their abilities to use, it's a safe bet they wouldn't have stayed.

You too may have a diamond-in-the-rough on your hands—if you're a perceptive observer and skilled enough to bring out your staff's multifaceted talents. Discuss your employees' goals in performance reviews or ask them periodically if they have a desire to learn new skills. To pinpoint the work employees might enjoy, ferret out as much as possible about their skills, background, education, activities, hobbies, and interests. The following questions will give you an idea of what to ask employees, either verbally or in a questionnaire. Tailor questions according to the employee's expressed interests.

- **Do you enjoy writing? (If their answer is "no," move on.) Do you write poetry or short stories? How would you describe your writing skills? Would you be willing to take a writing test? How long would it take you to write a 2,000-word feature story on this company? Describe your background or training. Do you believe with the right training the company could help you to improve your writing skills? Would you like to help write a company newsletter, sales and marketing materials, or customer correspondence?**

- **How do you feel about selling? (If their answer is "hate it," skip the following questions.) Do you believe you're a skilled salesperson? Are you a good listener? How would you rate your product knowledge? Confidence? What is the key to sales in your opinion? Describe your background or training. Do you believe with the right training the** company could help you to improve your sales skills? Would you like to take a stab at the sales department?

- Is researching fun? If you think so, how much experience do you have on the World Wide Web? Do you enjoy reviewing statistical data? If you were asked to determine why the company's defect rate has been increasing, how would you approach the problem? Do you enjoy looking for solutions to problems? Describe your research background or training. Do you consider yourself patient and persevering?

- Do you enjoy marketing? Do you enjoy analyzing demographics and statistical data? Have you ever conducted or designed a marketing research study? If you were told the company wanted to sell more products to baby boomers, would you be able to help us to determine how to accomplish our goal? What is key to successful public relations? How well do you understand the needs of media? What do you know about merchandising? Are you a creative person? Describe your fine art or computer design skills. Describe your marketing background and training. Do you believe with the right training the company could help you to improve your marketing skills?

- Does performing customer service give you great satisfaction? How would you rate your product knowledge? How would you describe your ability to listen? How well do you handle complaints? What would you do when a customer complains about slow service? How would you rate your communication skills? Describe your customer service background and training. Do you believe you could be trained to be a good customer service representative?

- Are you especially interested in human resources? Do you have experience reviewing résumés, interviewing, and hiring? What qualities would you look for when hiring someone to work for this company? How is your knowledge of 401(k) plans, pension plans, health insurance, and stock options? Do you enjoy paperwork? Describe your human resources background and training. Do you believe you could be trained to be a human resources representative?

- **How do you feel about information technology (IT)? Do you have knowledge of several computer software programs? Which ones? Do you know how to manipulate lots of raw data? If you were asked to tell us which customers have purchased more than $1,000 worth of merchandise in the past month, would you be able to generate the list? Could you manage the network? What computer industry magazines do you read? Describe your IT background and training. Do you believe you could be trained to be an IT professional?**

Are there other skills, hobbies, and activities that your employees enjoy, such as finance, accounting, manufacturing, or interior design? Industry-specific functions, such as cooking, drawing, drafting, engineering, or window dressing will also prove valuable.

To help employees test the difference between a whim and a career goal, have them help out in a new department where they feel they could be of use. When he was editor of *Chef* magazine, for example, the author of this book had a desire to create an educational conference to strengthen his publisher's industry trade show. The publisher was agreeable, and before long management responsibilities, challenges—and learning-curve anxieties—were added to the editing chores. Most important, though, conference organizing left this author feeling highly fulfilled and motivated, because he was able to utilize his latent management know-how, along with his communications and planning skills.

Since employees can't know in

YOU TOO MAY HAVE A DIAMOND-IN-THE-ROUGH ON YOUR HANDS—IF YOU'RE A PERCEPTIVE OBSERVER AND SKILLED ENOUGH TO BRING OUT YOUR STAFF'S MULTIFACETED TALENTS.

advance whether they will be happy in a new position, and you must have time to verify that the new staff member can pass muster, grant all transfers on a temporary basis. Tailor the tryout period to the complexity of the job and the amount of time required to learn it. For example, one employee might need only two weeks to figure out if he will enjoy sales work, while determining whether another will find a full-time writing position fulfilling might require two months. Only when both management and employee are satisfied should a job transfer become permanent, and a replacement for the vacated position found.

Give Employees Major Responsibilities

In the bustling kitchens of fine restaurants, the traditional chefs' hierarchy is a rigid and exacting arrangement. Complete with the culinary equivalent of generals, captains, and lieutenants, the chefs' "brigade system" mimics a military chain of command. Having evolved in nineteenth-century France, this system delegates precise responsibilities to each member of the kitchen staff, ensuring the efficiency, pride, and professionalism required to create a complex and artful meal.

You might think the brigade system was designed expressly for Charlie Trotter. From the very first chapter in this book, you've read how critical staff motivation is to Charlie Trotter's success. You've learned how Trotter challenges employees, encourages them, gives them growth opportunities, and allows them to do work they enjoy. And that's really only the tip of the iceberg. He also empowers them, takes great care in helping them plan their futures—and on the way to doing so, he gives employees major responsibilities.

Many entrepreneurs hold themselves responsible for most everything in the business. To be an effective leader, however, you'll need to shift several significant and challenging responsibilities to your employees. Responsibility motivates employees. It hooks them in, letting them "get under the skin" of your operation, erasing the distinction between their own interests and those of your business. Delegating these duties and burdens will not only motivate your staff members but also ease the pressure on you. Don't be afraid to give responsibilities early and often in an employee's career.

To take the first step in sharing key responsibilities, look at each member of your staff and determine which duties you'd like to entrust them with. Each role requires different qualities, personality, and experience, and you will need to match the right person with the right responsibility.

Most people are driven by the desire for power, authority, and independence. Even individuals who aren't leaders (and have no desire to be) at least need to have some decision-making authority and autonomy. That means all your staff members by nature want to be relatively self-directed and be trusted to make decisions. However, when challenged with greater responsibilities, some employees may oppose it at first. They may not want to be held accountable for anything extra, be it their coworkers, financial performance, hiring, new business, or development strategies. For many, just the idea of having such responsibilities is downright scary, so ease wary employees into additional duties.

Departmental management is the most obvious major responsibility you can provide a staff member. Appoint passionate, hard-working, detail-minded employees to positions of authority even before they think they're ready. Employees without previous management experience can head up small teams or departments of no more than five employees. Age should not be a reason to rule a candidate out. Even twentysomething staff members can be charged with the responsibility of managing administrative assistants or interns, for example. The individuals you pick to head departments need to know what it takes to get the job done in their area and which tasks each member of their team performs. They should generally be the hardest working employees in their groups, respected by their coworkers and charges.

Especially in small companies, you can appoint employees to manage certain business functions on a part-time basis, rather than outsource the work or handle it all yourself. If your company publishes a quarterly newsletter, for example, you clearly don't need a full-time editor or production manager. Simply make it one employee's responsibility to produce the newsletter. The person might not have to actually execute any of the work if he can encourage peers or superiors to write columns, pitch in with photography or design work, and handle production and printing. The added responsibility will test his resourcefulness and challenge him with increased accountability.

Certain key aspects of any business, such as marketing, human resources, and information technology, involve strategy, team building, planning, management, and supervision. If your company is small, you may not need full-time managers in each of these departments or disciplines, but they do lend themselves well to increased employee involvement.

Marketing consists largely of research, advertising, publicity, and sales. You could place one person in charge of the entire marketing effort, or put individuals in charge of each component. Certainly, heading up an entire marketing program can be a full-time job that requires extensive background and schooling. The individual aspects—including spearheading a market-research study, developing an advertising campaign, writing press releases, or setting sales goals—could be done part-time by carefully chosen employees with perhaps less training but with real interest or related experience.

Within a small firm, overseeing human resources is not usually a full-time job, but it cannot be overlooked. One or more managers can share responsibility for hiring, firing, and administering company benefits and guidelines. Train your managers to "hire for desire" and give them the responsibilities to help you develop a great staff by placing ads, reviewing résumés, interviewing, and hiring.

Information technology management is another great responsibility to assign the right individual. Naturally, this person must have experience in data management and computer technology, not to mention a strong desire to work with technology regularly. Responsibilities might include hardware and software price negotiation, equipment installation, software loading, list development, data retrieval, data security, network management, training employees to use the equipment, and crisis management.

Delegating for Success

If you're averse to risk, there are several conservative ways to distribute power to employees. When it comes to major shifts in policy or strategy, you can allow teams or groups of employees to arrive at decisions, reserving the right to approve any changes. You can also distribute power to employees in areas that don't affect your products or service, such as internal budgetary decisions. Bear in mind, though, that offering limited power and authority has limited motivational impact.

Naturally, autonomy is something employees should earn with hard work, adherence to your principles, dedication, and lots of desire. When you grant employees the autonomy to determine the best way to complete tasks, letting them find solutions on their own and operate with limited day-to-day direction, you provide them with a valuable dose of self-esteem. While your company doesn't have to implement every idea, let your staff map out the path.

As you begin to empower your staff, you need to make it clear what they can and cannot decide without your input. For starters, you need to tell employees that certain standards are immutable. If several are spelled out in the company handbook, remind them to consult it when in doubt. They cannot decide to take a day off without calling or wear shorts and a T-shirt to work if you require a shirt and tie, for example. Whenever possible, give them guidelines, such as dollar amounts, quantity limits, and time restraints.

One of the best guidelines of all is your company vision. Like your standards, the vision is not subject to change. Constantly remind staff members to refer to it when they are in a decision-making situation. Instruct them to ask themselves: Is this action consistent with the vision? Is there an alternative that would be better aligned with the vision? In this situation, am I compromising the vision simply to satisfy one customer or one employee? Could I satisfy the customer in another way without compromising the vision? Ultimately, they'll learn the parameters of their authority.

To achieve excellence and convince employees they play an important part in executing your vision, you need to give them the authority to do whatever it takes to deliver customer satisfaction and exceed expectations. That's why you should allow front-line employees to decide how to please dissatisfied customers and how to turn an ordinary experience into an extraordinary one. Whether it's a discount, a complimentary item, or an unexpected service, such as escorting customers to their cars two blocks away, the service people should call the shots. They're most in touch with customers, so they know better than you how to make it right—or more than right. "They're right there on the battle line," reasons Trotter. "They know what the guests' needs are, what their moods are, what's going well, what might go better, and what needs to be done to push it over the edge."

At Trotter's, for example, employees would never allow customers to light cigars in the restaurant, because that would negatively impact the enjoyment of other guests. Even if a smoker caused a scene or threatened to never return, employees know that everybody's excellent dining experience would be threatened by smoke drifting through the room. As a graceful solution, they might offer to buy the patron an after-dinner drink or a dessert, or suggest a nice jazz club nearby and pick up the cover charge.

Though it motivates them and gives them a sense of achievement, many employees won't always want to make decisions independently. Particularly when they're under deadline, they will often look for the easy way out. That's why you need to continuously encourage and even force them to be resourceful. For starters, don't always answer their questions. Rather than provide the solution, ask them questions to determine what resources they have and haven't tapped. Ask: Have you asked your coworkers for advice? What company materials or books have you consulted? What has the company done in situations similar to this? Have you made an educated guess?

Another great way to empower employees is to seek their input on company goals, strategies, and policies. Depending on the subject, you could convene a meeting of managers, administrative assistants, specific departments, or the entire company to make decisions. When it's time to set goals, ask for their thoughts. The next time you create a business development strategy, involve your staff. Before you offer summer hours, see what employees think. So long as you can reach a consensus, implement changes according to the group's decisions.

The decisions employees make don't always have to be about customer service, company policy, or strategy. Besides feeling that they make a difference in the business, your employees also need to feel that they're trusted. So give them budgetary limits and the authority to make independent decisions regarding business travel, equipment and supply purchases, and entertainment expenses.

Remember, you made an effort to hire honest, principled people, so you have no legitimate reason to distrust them.

Employees in account management and sales especially should be given an expense budget. Base your decision on where their clients are located and how many clients they have. When salespersons and account managers believe visits to out-of-state customers and prospects are necessary, they should be able to book reservations and go without permission. They also should be granted the authority to wine and dine a client to close a deal or to retain the business. Similarly, designers and marketing and communications employees should be allowed to order new computer software without a lot of red tape.

TO ACHIEVE EXCELLENCE AND CONVINCE EMPLOYEES THEY PLAY AN IMPORTANT PART IN EXECUTING YOUR VISION, YOU NEED TO GIVE THEM THE AUTHORITY TO DO WHATEVER IT TAKES TO DELIVER CUSTOMER SATISFACTION AND EXCEED EXPECTATIONS.

You and your staff have to work in the same space day in and day out, so ask the team for input when you make design or decorative changes to the office or place of business. At the very least, let them choose where their office or workspace will be. Particularly when it comes to office arrangement, employees will appreciate the fact that you value their opinions, because they are confident they know better than anyone what's best for them in terms of efficiency and camaraderie.

Whatever you do, you need to support their decisions more often than not. If you never agree with employees, implement their suggested changes, or support their on-the-spot decisions, they will be unmotivated and afraid to act in the future. Though they might not always do things the way you would, that doesn't necessarily mean they're making bad decisions. You have to be willing to do things a little differently on occasion and trust that your staff is equipped with the tools and training to troubleshoot effectively.

Remember Your Staff Is Human

"A person's errors are his portals of discovery," James Joyce once said. If you want to build an excellent staff, you have to let go and allow your employees to make their own decisions—and mistakes.

You're probably thinking that if you let staff people make decisions independently, they're bound to make wrong decisions occasionally. True. But chances are they won't make them frequently, because you have hired good people, trained them well, and brainwashed them with your vision, principles, and values. Beyond this concern, the motivational effect of empowerment far outweighs the risks of an occasional poor choice. What you need is the necessary confidence in your people and the tolerance for the inevitable mistakes that will be made now and again.

After indisputably bad decisions have been made, use the situation or incident as an opportunity to discuss your vision, standards, or company policies. Rather than embarrass individuals, discuss the decision privately or refer to it in a group setting, so long as it is not obvious who the guilty person is. Point out how and where the person went wrong, and with employee input try to determine what a good decision might have been.

Of course, where there's power, there's the possibility of abuse of power. As a result, don't be afraid to discipline employees who are careless, reckless, or undisciplined. The staff will not question why you reprimand a staff member for giving away hundreds of dollars in merchandise to a customer or writing the company newsletter in French rather than English. Because you hired good people and you take care of them in a number of ways, chances are they won't take advantage of their freedom. So take a chance and empower.

Prepare Employees for Their Futures,

Even If It Means They'll Move On

As a successful entrepreneur, self-actualization and self-fulfillment are key to your motivation. What about your employees? Like you, they need to feel that they're realizing their full potential. They want to believe that their capabilities, talents, skills, and experience will be put to use and that they'll fulfill their rightful destiny.

Charlie Trotter prepares his staff to be visionary managers, chefs, and restaurateurs, even if they don't hold those particular positions of authority at his restaurant. He knows this fulfills a need we all have: to grow and develop personally and professionally with an eye toward the future. Indeed, Trotter protégés such as Michael Smith and Debby Gold of Kansas City's American Restaurant, Guillermo Tellez of Miami's Mayya, and Rene Michelena of Boston's La Betola, today own or manage very successful restaurants.

As an exceptional leader, helping your employees advance will be an essential part of your own quest for excellence. In the words of Paul Hawken, CEO of the fine garden-supplies outlet Smith and Hawken: "The founder of a business gets to a point where his or her personal growth is much more involved with allowing others in the company to grow, so that they can give meaning to their own lives."

That's all fine and dandy, you might be saying, but shouldn't I hold onto employees whose training I've bankrolled? The answer is a little more complex than a simple "yes" or "no." Sure, every company requires a solid, stable core of specialists, technicians, and laborers, essentially people to execute the work. But as Trotter knows, by preparing individuals for futures in management, leadership, and ownership, they'll be highly motivated employees in the interim, when their opportunity for advancement arises.

Facing the Future

Let's face it: most of your employees don't intend to work for you forever. They also aspire to be better prepared, more diverse, higher skilled, more knowledgeable, better trained, and ultimately more successful when they leave your company than when they started. Helping them do so is not just a matter of altruism: if you want them to be happy and motivated members of your own workforce today, you need to help your employees to get to where they want to go, whether it's moving up in your organization or establishing themselves in another. Trotter recommends the following:

- **Create a generous tuition reimbursement program.**

- **Institute employee exchange programs.**

- **Buy the latest equipment and train your employees on it.**

- **Be a mentor to your employees.**

Create a generous tuition reimbursement program. Pay for advanced education if you really want to prepare employees for their futures. Despite the fact that the U.S. Congress has rolled back tax deductions for school-fee reimbursement, paying for further instruction and training is a good investment in your employees and in your company. Though $5,000 to $10,000 per year seems like a major investment, remember it motivates all employees, including those who aren't receiving the benefit directly. Everyone will be convinced that their employer really cares about the staff and its future.

First, investigate the costs of higher education in your community. It's not much of a motivator to offer employees $1,000 annually when it costs $15,000 per year to attend graduate business school, for example. You have hired individuals who are passionate about the business and interested in long-term careers in your industry. Encourage employees to attend industry trade shows, seminars, and conferences, not only for your company's benefit but also for theirs. Distribute memos to advise employees of upcoming educational opportunities, give them the time off to attend, and offer to pay for two or more conferences a year, for example. Most trade magazines list the best events in calendars with toll-free numbers and costs for your easy reference.

Institute employee exchange programs. Trotter knows that for industry-specific skills and knowledge, employee exchange programs with similar businesses are incredibly effective. Consequently, he often sends cooks to work in other excellent kitchens around the country, including Emeril's in New Orleans and Norman's in southern Florida. There, Trotter's people learn regional cooking techniques and apprentice with other culinary experts. Through such exchanges, employees become better motivated because they learn new methods and grow professionally. Sometimes they'll end up bringing the fruits of their experience back home.

Michelle Gayer started out at Trotter's seven years ago as a promising young cook straight out of culinary school. After a few years, Trotter decided that Gayer needed to expand her experience elsewhere—come what may. He arranged for her to bake with Nancy Silverton at Campanile and La Brea Bakery in Los Angeles. There Gayer remained until Trotter offered her the pastry chef position at his Las Vegas venue and finally back at Chicago headquarters. Soon after Gayer returned to the restaurant, Trotter began composing his *Charlie Trotter's Desserts* cookbook. He called upon Gayer's expertise in developing many of the recipes in the book; Gayer worked very closely with the editor, photographer, and at the ovens with Trotter himself. After the book was released, Trotter put Gayer through media training and the pastry chef became the restaurant's official representative and book-tour speaker.

To set up an employee exchange, call cooperative peer companies, both locally and nationally, and arrange for some of your employees to work for them for several days. Invite the companies to send a few of their staff to work for you.

Next time you plan to attend a conference in another city, take a few hard-working employees along and organize competitor visits in the area. At each business, ask staff members to identify five ways to improve the business. Then ask them to consider what they've learned that they can apply in their work and what about the experience will help them personally and professionally. It's a terrific learning experience for everybody involved.

Buy the latest equipment and train your employees on it. Whether or not all your employees need technological training to perform their jobs, you need to provide everyone with information-age skills and knowledge. That means training everybody to use computers and computer software, scanners, copiers, sorters, fax machines, and telephone systems. Line cooks at Charlie Trotter's

> "THE FOUNDER OF A BUSINESS GETS TO A POINT WHERE HIS OR HER PERSONAL GROWTH IS MUCH MORE INVOLVED WITH ALLOWING OTHERS IN THE COMPANY TO GROW, SO THAT THEY CAN GIVE MEANING TO THEIR OWN LIVES."
>
> — Paul Hawken,
> CEO, Smith and Hawken

don't need to know how to use a computer for their day-to-day tasks, but they will need to be computer literate if they ever hope to be a chef or restaurant owner. Knowing this, the head chef routinely assigns them data entry, word processing, and spreadsheet tasks and encourages them to explore the technology's capabilities on their own.

Remember, few workplace considerations discourage employees more than working with shoddy equipment and obsolete technology. Make an investment in advanced equipment, current technology, and research materials to give employees the tools they need. Buy the best machinery, lease and upgrade computers and software yearly, offer the best business magazines and industry trade publications in the employee lunchroom, and create a library of industry-related and general business books.

When your employees open their own businesses, they'll need to know how to locate and select vendors, negotiate with them, inspect their products, and demand better service. So it's important to teach employees how to develop relationships with vendors and to make equipment and supplies purchases. Besides cutting down on your workload, it will also help to educate and motivate your staff.

Be a mentor to your employees. In today's world, mentoring is a disappearing institution that can nevertheless inspire great loyalty and self-confidence in your employees. The best way to prepare employees is to teach them everything you know. Tell them what steps you took to prepare yourself to be an entrepreneur and continuously offer to support them in their career development. Recount details of your own experience and education: what you studied and learned, where you trained, who you approached for help and how they responded, which other businesses you researched, which books and journals you read, and how you conceived your own business.

While it's clear that everyone in your company can't be a leader, you should train your staff in the fundamentals and essentials of leadership. Teach them to inspire those around them with passion and enthusiasm, and how to model hard work and perseverance. Remind them by doing so that the best leaders are not afraid to roll up their sleeves and work with employees. Make sure they understand that leaders need to be the best they can, always trying to improve on the day before. Most important, tell staff members the best way to prepare for a leadership role is to adopt these behaviors today. They'll be prepared for their futures, whether they're with you or not.

Reward Employees

Generously, Frequently, and Unexpectedly

You've been there: you're an employee working your buns off, and now it's Christmas, or the end of the year, or near completion of the trickiest, most crucial project your company has had in a decade. Your boss tells you how much your efforts have been appreciated. When she mentions, her voice full of emotion, that she wants to reward your fine work with a small gift, you assume the recognition you deserve has finally arrived. Think again.

Who hasn't received trifling rewards over the years from employers? Maybe it was a half-percent pay raise, a $10 Christmas bonus, a flimsy pen and pencil set, or a movie-theater gift pass good only for Wednesday afternoon matinee performances. Do you remember how you felt each time? At best you thought these gifts were better than nothing. At worst you harbored far less generous thoughts about what your boss could do with such piddling gestures. Most unfortunate of all, these rewards had little or no positive impact on your performance. More than likely, they *demotivated* you.

Indeed, in too many businesses, the only rewards employees can hope for are modest pay raises begrudgingly doled out once a year. The real problem? Not only are such rewards rare and predictable, they're generally—and perhaps rightfully—seen by employees as entitlements rather than special recognition. If you expect rewards to have any distinguishable effect on employee motivation, you need to give them out unexpectedly, generously, and frequently. Don't fret: monthly pay raises and big cash bonuses are not the only way to go. Indeed there are many creative, thoughtful, and effective ways to reward people without giving them money.

Charlie Trotter believes it's important to reward his staff year-round for hard work, good attitude, long hours, dedication, and adherence to his principles. Many companies regularly put on competitions and reward employees for meeting and exceeding sales quotas, reaching efficiency or profitability targets, and nailing customer service measures. Typically, the rewards are cash bonuses or gifts such as televisions. But while these contests effectively spur employees to achieve company goals during a specific month or quarter, they cease to motivate employees once the contests are history.

Trotter doesn't want employees to perform well for particular events or clients, then slacken their pace with regular duties. He doesn't want them to give extra effort only in the months before their review, during a particularly busy season, or to win a contest. He wants his employees to perform with the same level of intensity and drive every day. To foster this behavior, he surprises them with random acts of generosity.

When considering how to revamp your employee rewards practices, keep these guidelines in mind:

- **Rather than trying to lure new employees in with big salaries, you should instead reward longevity and loyalty. At Charlie Trotter's, new hires don't see a raise for at least a year. After a year pay increases are** very fair; after a few years employees start to earn industry-leading salaries. Essentially, employees are expected to prove themselves for a couple of years before Trotter is willing to invest in them in a big way. Even when they start to earn good incomes, employees are motivated to stay at Charlie Trotter's and work hard since they know their efforts will be acknowledged and rewarded by the organization.

- Playing favorites when it comes to rewards is counterproductive. No matter what, never reward one employee and not another for the same quality work or service. Both the slighted worker and the gifted one will think you're just helping out your buddy, and neither will be motivated. Likewise, don't even consider giving one employee a larger prize than another for the same job. Word gets around, and you're inciting mutiny.

Giving the Gift That Motivates

There is an arsenal of rewards you can use to motivate high-performing, hard-working staff members. The opportunity to travel is a huge reward for most people, even when it's on work-related trips. Particularly if you travel to cosmopolitan cities, take employees along to help you with event management, speaking engagements, product demonstrations, site selection, and consulting projects. Most important, give them the time off to check out the sights, restaurants, clubs, cultural attractions, and sporting events. Rather than give a cash bonus, reward employees with a vacation to their favorite domestic or international destination. Using frequent flyer miles, Charlie Trotter has sent employees to Europe for rest and relaxation.

Your employees may be up to the gills in monogrammed pen and pencil sets, but plenty of other thoughtful gifts make a meaningful gesture. Trotter sometimes buys cooks a new chef's knife, chef's coat, bottle of wine, or culinary book to thank them for a particularly long or high-performance week. If you know your employees fairly well, buy them compact discs, books, cooking utensils, jewelry, silver, a watch, something you know they'll enjoy. Whatever you do, try to make the gift a surprise.

Employees with family responsibilities will get down on their knees and kiss your feet in return for flexible schedules, if your business permits you to offer them. You might even consider a four-day, full-time schedule for some employees. The key is to ask employees what schedule would be most rewarding to them. Trotter, for example, will arrange for cooks to report late and stay late occasionally (or routinely) if they have young children or a spouse they'd like to spend time with in the morning. Trotter himself prefers to start at noon so he can see his wife and son before going to work until 1 a.m.

Sometimes it's motivational to take things away from employees. No, I'm not talking privileges or perks here, but unwanted clerical or administrative tasks. Doing so will greatly assist hard-performing employees and leave them free to achieve in their areas of expertise. You can distribute their leftovers among several employees or hire interns to do the work. Ask high-performing staff members what tasks they'd like to unload, and do your best to relieve them. The more undesirable the work you take away, the greater effect the reward will have. Either way, you'll spend

TROTTER DOESN'T WANT EMPLOYEES TO PERFORM WELL FOR PARTICULAR EVENTS OR CLIENTS, THEN SLACKEN THEIR PACE WITH REGULAR DUTIES.... HE WANTS HIS EMPLOYEES TO PERFORM WITH THE SAME LEVEL OF INTENSITY AND DRIVE EVERY DAY. TO FOSTER THIS BEHAVIOR, HE SURPRISES THEM WITH RANDOM ACTS OF GENEROSITY.

hardly any money and these individuals will be motivated to work harder than ever.

If your business can support it, give model employees the opportunity to work from home at least one or two days a week—provided they consider it a reward. Thanks to modern technology, telecommuting is relatively simple to coordinate. All you need to do is pay to have staff members hooked up to the office with dedicated phone and fax lines, a computer modem, and an e-mail address, and provide other needed equipment and resources. You might even lease a computer for those who don't already own one.

At Trotter's, cooks are unable to do much work at home, because of the nature of their work. Others, such as the wine steward, office staff, and senior managers, are able to work part-time at home. Director of Marketing Mark Signorio does much of his design work in his home studio, for example. "That's what I love," says Signorio. "When I'm doing new designs I don't even come to work. I just present ideas to Charlie, drop them on his desk, and he calls me."

Collective outings, picnics, and holiday parties are other great ways to motivate the entire staff at once. Your company could have monthly staff meetings catered or convene meetings at a local restaurant. Even better, take your staff on group outings to baseball games or entertainment venues and organize a company picnic at least once a year in order to reward them for their hard work.

Other unconventional Trotter rewards have included cosigning on a school or car loan and even helping with a down payment on a house. Naturally, this is not a reward you want to offer to just anyone. You might reserve a reward like this for employees who have worked with you for at least three to five years and have shown genuine promise of staying with you for years to come.

Many employees believe they are entitled to benefits today, so how can you kick benefits up a notch? Reward your whole staff, as

Trotter does, by offering the best benefits in your field. Setting an industry standard for small independent restaurants, Charlie Trotter's provides a fully paid health-care and dental plan for employees, a 401(k) plan, to which employees contribute and the company matches a percentage of the funds, and a two- or three-week paid vacation—absolutely unheard of in the industry. Far less common but very worthwhile benefits you could consider are major life insurance plans, profit sharing, and pensions.

When it comes time for raises, do it with verve. Don't just hand them out in the conventionally impersonal, lackluster manner. Instead, give your valued staff a real thrill by surprising them. At Charlie Trotter's, recipients learn about their raises when they open their pay envelopes. Enclosed with the increased paycheck is a note reading, "Just to acknowledge the great job you've been doing, we've increased your salary."

To sufficiently motivate employees, pay increases after one or two years of employment should be at least 10 percent of income and as much as 20 percent or 30 percent when job responsibilities increase significantly. Unless you want to kill their motivation entirely, never tell staff members, "I'm sorry, I can't afford to give you a sizable raise because you already earn a high salary." If you feel an employee's work or performance is inadequate, say so. If not, find the means to give them what they deserve. Income level should reflect how hard they have worked over a number of years, whether it was for you or someone else.

Bonuses also make great rewards for hard work and performance, but be careful to tailor them to a person's income. A thousand-dollar bonus given to an individual making $30,000 a year is a far more meaningful reward than the same bonus given to an employee earning $100,000. Do it right, and you'll get the performance you seek. Bonuses equal to 5 percent of annual income are quite generous.

It's also best to offer monthly or quarterly bonuses and tie them to profitability, as Trotter does. The chef has recognized over time that short-term goals are stronger motivators for employees than yearly targets. Bonuses linked to profitability also force his staff members to watch costs while they are trying to generate higher revenues. Moreover, frequent bonuses allow him to adjust the quotas, goals, and targets quickly and easily when the business environment changes.

innovating

FOR EXCELLENCE

Create Challenges

for Yourself and Your Business

"In the long run, you hit only what you aim at. Therefore, though you should fail immediately, you had better aim at something high."

—HENRY DAVID THOREAU

In the early 1900s, Henry Ford put forth an audacious goal: to democratize the automobile; to put it within the reach of everyone, from the wealthy to ordinary working people.

In the 1950s, following the war, Sony Electronics executives set out to make their company best known for changing the worldwide poor-quality image of Japanese projects.

In the 1960s, Boeing CEOs set the goal of becoming the dominant player in commercial aircraft and bringing the world into the jet age.

The lesson? The monumental challenges these leaders set for themselves and their companies energized generations of workers and allowed history to be made.

In major corporations and in small business, only a challenged and motivated leader can effectively spur employees to strive for excellence. For you, self-challenge must become a way of life.

Many entrepreneurs, basking in the reputations of their successful, highly regarded companies, become overconfident and then complacent. Resting on their laurels, they lose sight of the vision that inspired them in the first place, and excellence begins to erode. Glamorous, celebrated eateries are among the worst offenders: "A lot of restaurants reach a point at the top and they just coast," says Charlie Trotter's former Chef de Cuisine Guillermo Tellez. "Charlie doesn't want to do that. He won't get comfortable."

Clients, peers, and competitors will challenge you from time to time, but that's not enough. "You can have a hero, you can look to somebody who inspires you, but ultimately you have to continue to devise ways to motivate yourself and to keep things interesting for yourself," explains Trotter.

The greatest way to challenge yourself is to constantly change what you do. Few entrepreneurs are better than Charlie Trotter at challenging themselves. One of the most interesting ways he does this is to change the restaurant's menu every day. Along with providing an everyday adventure for customers, the constant change is largely intended to keep Trotter, the staff, and the menu exceptionally fresh.

Obviously, if customers count on your paint company or hardware store supplying very specific brand-name materials, tools, or product models, the notion of changing these regularly doesn't make sense. You can, however, change other aspects of your business. Look for different ways to execute your work, identify new methods to organize, supervise, and monitor tasks and projects, and continuously develop new company tactics and strategies.

Rare is the person who can superbly perform the same work day in and day out for years. So don't count on that person being you. Instead, to keep highly motivated, hunt for new tasks you can perform as part of your everyday job. Charlie Trotter stays "wired" by not only cooking, but also hiring employees, writing the restaurant's menu, training and managing staff, carrying out public relations, and hosting a PBS television program. Challenge yourself to learn new functions, such as communications, marketing, and public relations. Your motivation will heighten and you'll save yourself money in the process by becoming your own best consultant in key areas of business.

One of Trotter's greatest self-administered challenges, for ex- ample, is to dazzle the world's demanding diners. One such customer is Steve Greystone, a world traveler who's dined at the most sublime restaurants from Paris to Milan. Greystone's presence in the dining room excites the chef like no one else. Why? "I get most excited by the most discerning client," admits Trotter. "To me it's the ultimate challenge. I'm testing my mettle, finding out what I'm made of. If we can blow him away with a particular offering, it lets me know we are capable of doing something at the most refined

"I GET MOST EXCITED BY THE MOST DISCERNING CLIENT," ADMITS TROTTER. "TO ME IT'S THE ULTIMATE CHALLENGE. I'M TESTING MY METTLE, FINDING OUT WHAT I'M MADE OF. IF WE CAN BLOW HIM AWAY WITH A PARTICULAR OFFERING, IT LETS ME KNOW WE ARE CAPABLE OF DOING SOMETHING AT THE MOST REFINED LEVEL."

level." Every business has customers who are very discriminating, hard to please, or just plain difficult. Pinpoint what it is that makes these clients happy. Then challenge yourself and your employees to deliver an ecstatic experience. Perhaps the customer expects to be pampered, receive a nearly split-second response to phone calls, or have lifetime guarantees on product purchases. Consider these demands a challenge. Rather than getting in a huff and telling such demanding types to take a hike, give them what they want and then some.

Another challenge for entrepreneurs is to attempt to satisfy *all* customers, even those who rarely ever patronize your business or businesses like yours. If necessary, ask your employees to spend more time working with such customers to explain your services or to share knowledge about product features. If that customer is unaccustomed to spending as much as you're charging for a product, try providing even more value than usual.

The thrill of challenge is why culinary neophytes excite Trotter, too. Frequently, first-time diners come to Charlie Trotter's to celebrate their proudest achievements: a fiftieth wedding anniversary, a major job promotion. Many of these customers are not particularly wealthy or knowledgeable about fine cooking, but the evening is tremendously important to them and costs far more than what they usually spend to dine. Trotter considers it a great honor they've chosen his restaurant and moves mountains to make the dining experience the most memorable they have ever had.

Entrepreneurs who really need a serious challenge can try what may be the most trying of all: making model staff of employees who are one violation away from a pink slip. Because you hired them, they must have had the fire and desire initially. Challenge yourself to figure out what happened. Speak with them in person, take them out to lunch or dinner, work with them one-on-one, take them under your wing, and push them to excel.

You'll also motivate yourself by setting challenging performance and efficiency goals for yourself and your business. For starters, continuously set new and hard-to-achieve sales, revenue, and profit goals. Perhaps you can shoot for higher market share, higher traffic, or improved customer service, measured by a research study. It's always smart to work on your company's efficiency, too. Find ways to handle more customers at once, discover faster methods to take orders and manufacture and deliver products, plus hunt for ways to conserve energy and raw materials.

Set your sights on prestigious industry awards both for personal and company accomplishments. Many trade, business, and professional associations, trade magazines, consumer magazines, foundations, and academies offer awards both for outstanding individual and company performance. Find out what awards are available by reading your industry's major trade magazines. At your local library, consult the *Encyclopedia of Associations* (Gale Research) and the Bacon's Directories of magazines, newspapers, TV, and radio media (in print and CD-ROM) to locate the contact information you'll need.

Next, gather the entry forms for several industry awards and study what it takes to be nominated. While it's best to shoot for awards that are challenging, don't pick accolades that are way out of your league. Talk about potential awards all the time with your staff: let them know what the goal is and what it's going to take to get there. Once you win one award, shoot for others.

Stay a step ahead of yourself so you don't become complacent. Once you complete all these steps, challenge yourself to find *new* ways to challenge yourself.

Most great leaders, like Charlie Trotter, continuously chart new mountains to climb for themselves and their followers. Trotter's has earned four stars from every Chicago newspaper and magazine, plus five stars from *Mobil Guide* and five diamonds from AAA. The restaurant has twice been named the best restaurant in the world for food and wine by *Wine Spectator;* Trotter's has also been inducted into the international Relais and Chateaux. Trotter himself has been nominated Chef of the Year five times by the James Beard Foundation (an award which he won in 1999), best chef in the United States by *Wine Spectator,* and best chef in the Midwest by the James Beard Foundation.

Is he satisfied? (What do you think?) The restaurant's current goals are to receive the James Beard Foundation's Award for Outstanding Service and the Malcolm Baldrige Award for excellence—which no small business has ever won. If the restaurant accomplishes these feats, Trotter won't be sitting around drinking champagne and waxing nostalgic. He'll be back at the board, planning new schemes to motivate himself and his troops.

Create an Environment Where Innovation Is Possible

"The concept is interesting and well formed," a Yale University management professor told student Fred Smith regarding his paper proposing reliable overnight delivery service. But in order to earn a grade of C or better, "the idea must be feasible." Smith went on to found a company several years later known as Federal Express.

When it comes to innovation, Charlie Trotter knows that keeping an open mind is essential to the development of an excellent business. For many hard-working entrepreneurs, however, the notion of innovation is not a comfortable one. The term itself conjures up lofty historic images of landmark inventions: the printing press, lightbulb, airplane, computer. And most practical businessmen—with the exception of, say, a software honcho with a well-funded R&D team—know that their workers don't have the time, training, or wherewithal to dream of such goals.

No need to panic, though. Innovations don't have to be momentous technological breakthroughs. Instead, they can be small, subtle moves that ultimately fortify your company's overall level of excellence, as Trotter has discovered time and time again.

"Charlie Trotter's restaurant is distinguished most by its culinary innovation," says Phil Vettel of the *Chicago Tribune,* "the constant fiddling with recipes and introduction of new ingredients." Indeed, meeting Charlie Trotter's most remarkable goal—"Never serve the exact same food preparation twice"—chefs there have created a staggering 50,000 distinctive dishes over the course of more than 3,000 nights of service. It requires that every single day he and the staff develop entirely new product combinations, finding new ways to season, prepare, present, and serve the food.

It's not surprising that jazz and classical music fan Trotter (named, incidentally, after Charlie Parker) calls his PBS cooking series "The Kitchen Sessions with Charlie Trotter": the chef takes very seriously the parallels between the work and music. "To be a significant musician, you have to be greatly disciplined, you have to understand the history of the music and how the elements go together. What I so admire about performers like Miles Davis and Charlie Parker is their ability to *improvise,* to look at something and interpret it one way today, and reinterpret it differently tomorrow. That's why, as a chef, I've looked at those people as models. Think of Miles Davis playing 'My Funny Valentine.' I hear it one way, then again in a different way, and again in a different way. He's always emphasizing something different. We do something like that with our food. It's not just change for the sake of change; there has to be a foundation to it, there has to be an understanding of historical ideas, flavors, and textures." If Charlie Trotter's is one of the nation's most successful eateries, it's because the chef-owner has created a *culture of innovation* in which nearly all employee ideas are considered.

Getting the Ideas Out There

Virtually any business or team of individuals can innovate. As a manager, all you have to do is to give your ego a time-out and get out of the way. Remember, more than likely, you're not going to be the one to conceive of most of the earthshaking ideas. What you need to do is create a business in which ideas from employees and outsiders—including customers, family, friends, and industry experts—are encouraged, welcomed, and implemented.

Consider legendary investor and mutual fund manager Peter Lynch, whose investment strategies have become the model of this open-minded approach to innovation. According to Lynch himself, many of his most profitable investment inspirations during the over twenty years he spent managing the Fidelity Magellan Fund came from the seemingly most quotidian of sources—sources such as the shopping habits of his own family.

Your staff is on the front lines. It is they who are most in touch with customers—and they who are able to recognize opportunities that you don't. Unfortunately, few entrepreneurs actually ask for employee recommendations regarding business operations. When they do, they ask only senior staff. No matter what, encourage every employee to continually offer their input. Ask all your staff members to share their observations and ideas immediately with a manager or with you. Doing so creates a culture where innovation can thrive.

Challenge yourself and your staff to innovate constantly. Demand that a set number of new products be introduced each year and that particular product designs be scrapped and reinvented each year. In addition, ask employees to develop a set number of new tools and software to help them to perform their work.

Innovations are often simply new or improved ideas, methods, or devices. Though it might not make the *Wall Street Journal,* for example, rearranging the tables in a restaurant to add a greater number of seats would rank as an important discovery.

Sometimes, an innovation can be a small, esthetic improvement that subtly upgrades a business's ambiance or level of refinement. To conclude each meal at Charlie Trotter's, for instance, guests are served complimentary *mignardises,* small, finely wrought chocolate candies crafted in-house. After an eight-course meal, however, Trotter's diners are often just too full to sample the delectable sweets, and instead wish to take them home. Until recently, the waitstaff simply wrapped the *mignardises* in aluminum foil and returned them to the departing guest—a practical but inelegant solution. Last winter, however, at a group meeting, a waiter suggested that a small box would make a more fitting take-home container for the sweets. Charlie agreed and assigned a server the task of finding one. First, the waiter brought back stock-type gold-foil boxes to use. Later, fancier monogrammed versions with padding and inserts took their place. Ultimately, Trotter's located carved wooden boxes from Thailand, then had them imprinted with the restaurant's own logo. Today, these have become collector's items and, of course, a charming end to an extraordinary evening.

Be willing to listen to employee complaints: important innovations can come in the form of changes in compensation, hiring, training, and team building that ultimately affect products and service dramatically. Employee gripes about pay, for example, are common, but often repressed. Real innovators like Trotter search for solutions to these questions, turning to employees for answers.

At Trotter's, the waitstaff spoke up several years ago, saying they would feel secure if their pay fluctuated less. Their complaint was legitimate. In the restaurant business, due to variations in customer traffic, pay for service staff is traditionally inconsistent. Instead of telling his employees to grin and bear it—ultimately causing resentment and enmity—Trotter developed a revolutionary compensation method: today, his waitstaff are on salary, even though customers continue to leave gratuities for their services. After guests leave, the restaurant collects all the gratuities and redistributes them in the form of salaries with full benefits. Ultimately, the waitstaff makes at least as much money, and "night-by-night" financial worries have been eliminated. "I don't like the idea of grubbing for money every night at every table," explains Trotter. "Why not treat it like a profession? This way, they know they're going to earn x amount a week, x amount a year." Customer service is greatly improved, because customer stereotypes—preconceptions about who's likely to leave a big tip, who's not—no longer influence staff performance. Also, because these employees earn a specific annual income, they are more motivated and loyal than if compensation were unstable.

To encourage employees to offer ideas regularly, it's important to provide a forum, some direction, and the free time. As Trotter does, you might distribute questionnaires every month to staff members, asking them to write out their ideas, to spur their creative thinking. For example, you might ask them to list at least one new way to reorganize

"WHAT I SO ADMIRE ABOUT PERFORMERS LIKE MILES DAVIS AND CHARLIE PARKER IS THEIR ABILITY TO **IMPRO-VISE,** TO LOOK AT SOMETHING AND INTERPRET IT ONE WAY TODAY, AND REINTERPRET IT DIFFERENTLY TOMORROW. THAT'S WHY, AS A CHEF, I'VE LOOKED AT THOSE PEOPLE AS MODELS."

— Charlie Trotter

the storage area, work area, and display counters, or identify one bottleneck in work flow and consider two new ways to eliminate the problem. Trotter also convenes a staff meeting every day, which lasts approximately half an hour, in which the staff brainstorms for at least ten to fifteen minutes about ways to improve and innovate. Plan meetings with some or all of your own staff, during which you present them with a subject, such as "sales presentation," and ask them to think of several completely new approaches.

To ensure everyone is involved in brainstorming sessions, randomly ask quiet staff persons to contribute. It's also important to constantly point out that no ideas are stupid and make sure employees don't scoff at their peers' ideas, no matter how tempting it may be to do so.

Don't make knee-jerk negative judgments if you hope to be able to innovate with any regularity. Clearly, new product ideas require some research and development, which could be a significant investment. But be willing to give most ideas a chance, so long as they're not outrageously costly to implement. Most new methods and process changes aren't terribly risky, so implement them as often as possible. Whatever you do, be very positive about their chances for success to make sure everyone is trying hard to make the idea work.

You want to convince employees you're giving their ideas every chance for success. Few accomplishments are more fulfilling for a staff member than the opportunity to present an idea and see it implemented. On the flip side, it's very demotivating to ask employees for their contributions and never use them or to attempt to implement them without sufficient resources. Your employees will be more likely to innovate when you implement their ideas and back them with human resources as well as capital.

"At the restaurant, all new ideas are given consideration," says Controller Judi Carle. "If an idea is not acted upon, you're given a reason. It may be that it's not cost-effective, or that it would adversely affect another department. Or maybe we're not ready for it just yet. But whether the idea is put into practice or not, there's no fear of being told it's a stupid idea, or being looked at in a negative way. One thing Charlie is very clear about is that any idea has merit. An idea that doesn't work right now may be the basis of a great project a year from now."

Move quickly and decisively when it comes to implementation, because the fearlessness you display emboldens employees to come up with additional ideas and convinces them you are "wild" about innovation. The last thing staff members want is for their ideas to languish in your indecisive mind for months at a time. "I sometimes throw caution to the wind," admits Trotter. "When I have an idea or if a new idea is presented, I'm prepared to implement it instantly." Most important, thank employees for their ideas—even when they're not useful. When employees submit impractical suggestions, Trotter encourages them to continue to offer recommendations every day thereafter.

Finally, put your money where your mouth is: reward big ideas with big cash bonuses. You should reward employees a cut of the sales on new product ideas. Give them handsome bonuses for new gadgets that help staff members to perform their jobs, and offer incentives for new processes or methods. The rewards will convince employees how serious you are about innovation and will encourage them to consider new ideas, methods, and products all the time.

27 Innovators Hunt for External Opportunities

In the early 1300s, on a quest for the wondrous and the unknown, Venetian adventurer Marco Polo made his way along the rubbled Silk Road and beyond to faraway Asia. His travels would take him through Persia, Malacca, and the kingdoms of the great Khans, and finally to the court of the Emperor of China. Polo returned home years later with tales—sometimes rather florid exaggerations—of the marvels he'd seen. He also brought back strange Eastern culinary inventions, such as the noodle, to the delight of Venetian cooks. In the following centuries, English, Spanish, and Portuguese explorers gleaned other exotic finds from the New World: maize, tomatoes, *chocolatl.* The concoctions invented from these novel ingredients became mainstays in European cuisine.

Such a spirit of exploration (albeit with a touch less romance) will stand your business in good stead. It's important that you foster a company culture that spurs you and your employees to search for innovative opportunities in the world around you. Innovations can satisfy needs that are unmet or offer solutions to time-worn problems, or they can be new ways of saving time, space, and money.

Once you learn to recognize opportunities, innovative ideas will come fairly easily. Your employees may be the ones to conceive innovative methods, ideas, and products, but your direction is crucial. You'll pose questions, send them down the right paths, share innovative opportunities, and discuss consumer trends with them.

Prepping the Search Party

To ferret out innovative opportunities, you and your employees should begin to study both local and national public opinion. Subscribe to and read a variety of newspapers, consumer magazines, and industry trade publications to learn what buyers and users think. The *Wall Street Journal, Fortune* and *Forbes* magazines, the *New York Times,* the *Chicago Tribune,* the *Los Angeles Times, U.S. News & World Report, American Demographics,* specialty magazines (such as *Architectural Digest* and *Food & Wine*), and industry trade publications routinely present and analyze consumer perception and opinion studies better than anyone else. You'll find reports on such topics as consumer attraction to and fear of technology and consumer interest in the environment, nutrition, spirituality, fitness, education, personal finances, safety, health care, and retirement.

Begin to assemble a library of your own. You and your staff should read articles regularly, highlight key information, clip the most illuminating pieces and circulate them around the office, and file them for future reference. All the while, look for patterns, consistencies, discrepancies, similarities, and differences.

Some of the best innovative opportunities can be unearthed if you and your employees study consumer activities, hobbies, and interests. When you're reading some of the aforementioned publications, try to find answers to questions like these: Nationwide, what are the most popular sports, fitness, and recreational activities today? Is attendance up at art museums? What do young adults do for entertainment? What hobbies are big? How many people cook, garden, and make home repairs? What are today's hottest foods and cuisines? Where are people traveling? What kind of music is big?

Search for the facts that will expose high-growth markets. For Trotter and his fellow restaurateurs, this includes statistics such as the percentage of meals eaten away from the home—now more than 50 percent and growing. Ethnic cuisines, such as Pan-Asian and Nuevo Latino, are among the most popular in the United States. Other entrepreneurs look at sports and technology trends such as the fact that thrill-seeking in general and extreme sports such as hang gliding, skydiving, rock climbing, and bungee jumping have soared in popularity over the last decade. Or that the number of people purchasing products via the Internet is burgeoning.

When you read about major consumer trends, ask yourself and your employees: What can we learn from this information? Is it possible to predict future trends based on this information? Do some of these trends converge? What could the business do to capitalize on these trends? Could we rethink the way we design, process, package, merchandise, promote, and sell our products? What kinds of products might fit these trends? Are there completely new products or services we could create?

While it's very important to examine consumer opinions, be warned they're not always consistent with action. The area of nutrition and fitness is a prime example. Despite the current professed interest in healthful cuisine and aerobic exercise, today there are more obese Americans than ever before. Studies show that, when speaking with a researcher, we tend to exaggerate the amount of exercise we do and hide the amount of high-fat foods we consume. Similarly, there are far more Americans who claim they want to protect the environment than U.S. consumers who purchase organic foods and other earth-

IT'S IMPORTANT THAT YOU FOSTER A COMPANY CULTURE THAT SPURS YOU AND YOUR EMPLOYEES TO SEARCH FOR INNOVATIVE OPPORTUNITIES IN THE WORLD AROUND YOU. INNOVATIONS CAN SATISFY NEEDS THAT ARE UNMET OR OFFER SOLUTIONS TO TIME-WORN PROBLEMS, OR THEY CAN BE NEW WAYS OF SAVING TIME, SPACE, AND MONEY.

friendly products. Because you want to be sure there's a bona fide opportunity, your business plan will need to take into account the incongruity between public opinion polls and customer purchasing habits before you innovate. Consider the when, what, where, why, and how of buying patterns, in conjunction with consumer price sensitivity. To find the answers, seek out data from trade associations and read trade journals.

To be a successful innovator, you also need to think about the shifting demographics in the world around you. According to U.S. demographers, the most significant changes in the upcoming decades will be an upsurge in the number of Hispanic and Asian Americans and a tidal wave of aging baby boomers. In the years ahead, keep your eyes and ears open for shifts in income levels in your neighborhood and region of the country, changes in level of education (college degrees could become less common because of runaway costs), new occupations that spring up as a result of the information age, and the stratification of social classes. All of these will affect purchasing trends.

To find out what these demographic shifts will mean for your business, stay in close contact with your customers. Besides asking them for innovative ideas, you and your employees need to listen to and watch for the clues your customers provide. Case in point: knowing the number of vegetarians was mushrooming nationwide, Charlie Trotter's has always offered creative vegetable and grain-based dishes. Over time, Chef Trotter observed something less apparent: a significant number of health-conscious diners ordering his meat-free cooking, it turned out, weren't necessarily vegetarians. Because the response to these menu items was so positive, Trotter began to offer a full seven-course, meat-free tasting menu. Owing to its success, he decided to write the *Charlie Trotter's Vegetables* cookbook, one of the most comprehensive, sophisticated—and popular—studies written on modern vegetable cooking.

Trotter regularly makes an appearance in the dining room to speak with his customers and to ask them if they are enjoying their meal and the service. He also notes the casual references and comments they make: an increasing interest in East Indian cuisine; a state-of-the-art software program just purchased; a recent trip to the Caribbean; the soccer game broadcast that afternoon; a common gastrointestinal disorder requiring a fat-restricted diet. Cumulatively, these comments often lead to major innovative business ideas.

Linking Up for Innovation

Another possibility for expanding your company's horizons is to consider a partnership with other companies. Of course, following a course of this magnitude will require much thought and consideration, not to mention information and planning.

When Trotter decided his firm's future would have to involve partnering with other companies, he knew the links should not be haphazard. In his mind there had to be a natural, organic connection between his and a partner company, and that any partner would have to match his exceptionally high standards. In 1996, Trotter approached two Chicago-based operations, Chicago Cutlery and Sara Lee Bakery, suggesting several different and mutually beneficial ways for becoming partners. At the time, both companies declined the offers. Within a year, however, both had called Trotter back, proposing the same projects. Chicago Cutlery developed a line of Charlie Trotter Knives, with Chef Trotter as company spokesman, and Sara Lee sponsored the first thirteen episodes of Trotter's PBS cooking show.

The Wide World of Opportunity

As Marco Polo and his ilk have proven, travel can put you face to face with some of the most exciting raw material for innovation. Next time you're in Tokyo, Paris, Sao Paolo, or Peoria, take a close look at what people are wearing, which brand of vehicle they're driving, what they're eating or talking about, which books they're reading. Find out where they're hanging out and spending family time. All of this can inspire compelling new ideas.

Charlie Trotter recently made a trip to the Pacific Islands and returned to Chicago fervent about the food ingredients he encountered there. "Sure enough, we were served Polynesian fare when he returned," says long-time customer Dick Berger. Taro root, star fruit, galanga, and coconut-based sauces for meat and seafood dishes became some of the starring elements. "He incorporated the new flavors overnight. I can just imagine Charlie in the islands," laughs Berger. "'I'll have to try this back at the restaurant!'"

Allow Employees to Own Their Innovative Ideas 28

You and your staff have worked up a number of brilliantly innovative ideas, thanks to an organizational culture that promotes employee input and careful analysis of the business environment in which you live. Now it's time to make these ideas a reality by allowing employees to "own" their ideas and implement them themselves. Think about it logically: the resident genius who dreamed up an idea is the person most confident that it will succeed. For most, pride in potential achievement will fuel performance. And because nobody wants to be embarrassed by failing, there's a built-in incentive to make sure the concept is implemented properly.

No matter how simple a new method, idea, or product is, executing it generally requires human labor and know-how. Have your innovators sit down and work out the nuts and bolts of bringing new projects to life: How many new employees will be needed? How permanently? How many veteran employees will require additional training? Does the R&D process require staff with special qualifications? If so, how many of our employees have the right stuff?

Next, ask your idea-generators to consider what additional research materials, supplies, and equipment their projects require: Will new packaging be needed? What specific tools, machinery, or equipment would allow us to implement the methods easily? What kind of workstations will we need? What new computer software or hardware will we need to manufacture the products or implement the processes?

Before creating a new product, be sure to determine if other companies have beaten you to the punch. You and your innovators should closely evaluate other market entries to be sure yours will be the best on the block. Look for flaws, poor craftsmanship, defects, shortcomings, inferior components, and styling problems. This kind of early-stage comparison and subsequent revamping of your product can save you thousands of dollars later on and enable you to establish a dominant market position.

To market novel products or ideas you need to know when they will be ready for public debut. Ask your staff innovators to develop an approximate timetable and set a target date for each product or idea launch. They should begin by asking both you and their peers for historical data, then continue the research off-site. Once they've amassed their data, have them estimate the length of time needed to do the following:

- **Research the idea from start to finish**

- **Hire and train specialists, if necessary, to research and develop the innovation**

- **Obtain and set up the equipment and supplies necessary to produce the product or implement the method**

- **Train current employees to use the new equipment or method**

- **Manufacture an alpha version of the product for testing and then a beta version for launch**

After your innovators have identified the type of human resources, equipment, and supplies required and established production schedules, ask them to calculate the approximate project costs. They can consult industry trade associations and magazines to determine average salaries for skilled workers, such as marketing managers, engineers, chefs, graphic artists, or machine operators. For equipment and supplies estimates, have staff members refer to manufacturers' lists (even though your management staff may well be able to negotiate a lower price later). Before you start seeing stars—don't get too worried: you may already have most of the resources on hand. In fact, many innovations don't require new hires, equipment, and supplies purchases at all.

When it's time to put ideas to the test, have your idea-generating employees develop prototype products or implement their new method or idea on a small scale to determine viability. After they've done so, evaluate their work, then send them back to the drawing board with suggestions for changes and additions. Once you're happy with their ideas, products, or methods, they should ask a random sample of customers to evaluate them. Remember that every

THINK ABOUT IT LOGICALLY: THE RESIDENT GENIUS WHO DREAMED UP AN IDEA IS THE PERSON MOST CONFIDENT THAT IT WILL SUCCEED. FOR MOST, PRIDE IN POTENTIAL ACHIEVEMENT WILL FUEL PERFORMANCE.

product, method, and idea needs to reflect your values and vision of excellence.

When you are satisfied that the innovations are of excellent quality, give employees the green light to bring their ideas to life in full force. Let them announce their results to the company, demonstrate how the innovations work, and train their colleagues. Let the innovators manage the transition from old to new methods, since they'll know the obstacles and challenges and what steps are needed to get the job done.

As often as possible, the individual who has conceived of an innovative idea should head up the research and development team, sharing their vision for the product, idea, or method with team members and taking responsibility for deadlines and quality of execution. This is a great way to motivate all your employees to innovate, because they know they'll be rewarded with management of an important project.

While it may be inappropriate to put an intern or new hire in charge of a major product innovation, most regular staff members are capable of carrying out that duty. Due to their insider's awareness, they can also be entrusted to select colleagues as team members, because they know their peers' skills and capabilities as well as anyone. (When it comes time to hire outsiders, however, keep yourself involved in the selection process.)

While many idea generators won't have the skills or the training to write advertising copy or develop research studies, most will be able to make solid contributions to their project's marketing message and positioning. Why? Your innovators probably had a target market in mind when they thought of their ideas. Invariably, the inspiration was based on a knowledge of consumer tastes, interests, activities, and hobbies as well as customer purchasing habits and demographics. Specifically, as designers, innovators can help distinguish product features and can testify from experience about the benefits and rewards associated with product usage. Moreover, they often will have already thought of catchy names and creative packaging concepts while developing the products.

Though most people will automatically monitor the success of their own innovations, you should formalize this process. Whether the product is a baseball bat, baby blanket, or a baguette, your innovators should track customer satisfaction and measure sales. Have them monitor changes in efficiency, accuracy, production capacity, number of defects, product loss and quality, and most important, customer satisfaction. It's crucial for the innovators to take part in this step, because having developed the products or services, they may see solutions or enhancements others don't. Once your innovators evaluate profit and loss and measure customer satisfaction, they'll be able to report back on the effectiveness of promotion and the amount of sales.

Act Quickly, 29

Because the Problem with Instant

Gratification Is It Takes Too Long

In the wee hours of the morning, a pair of your most creative employees enter your office, an hour before their shift begins. Their hair is disheveled, their eyes are red and shining like a lunatic's. They've been up all night, they tell you, haunted by a brilliant new idea for the company. The minute you hear it, you know they're onto something. The discussion grows animated. It spurs new visions of your own. You can virtually *feel* excellence in the making. The moment they leave, you prepare to make calls, rally your troops, and put the concept into action.

Somehow, though, tiny doubts creep in. A minute passes. You hang up the receiver. I'll think about it tomorrow, you promise yourself. Next week. As the days pass, it becomes easier to simply tackle old business, known quantities. The vision hovers on the edge of oblivion, in grave danger of vanishing.

What are you waiting for? To be struck by lightning?

"Paralysis by analysis" is indeed the bane of many small and large businesses. To avoid its deadly clutches, quit thinking, analyzing, evaluating, calculating, doubting, and fearing, and start doing. Whether you have faith in a higher power or simply your employees and yourself, you need to trust it and take action. Immediately. Remember: once you've identified opportunities and give innovations all the energy and drive you can muster, chances are good they'll succeed. Charlie Trotter operates this way nonstop.

"When Charlie decides he wants to do something," says Judi Carle, "he means now. One Wednesday, I recall, he decided to start a brand new cookbook on meat and game. By the following Tuesday, we had shot the first eight photos. That's not an anomaly. It's just a way of life." This policy of rapid innovation invigorates employees. "When you work for a really big company, everything is done by committee and everything takes a long time," says Trotter's longtime pastry chef Michelle Gayer. "At Charlie Trotter's, decisions—good or bad—are made quickly. You get things done, you get going. It makes you feel like you're part of something really special."

Most research studies, reports, and other bureaucratic red tape focus too much on the reasons why you *shouldn't* innovate. You don't have all the time in the world. Facts are facts: innovation is possible if you move quickly once ideas are presented. Your staff isn't going to bother to present new ideas if those ideas are rarely implemented— or if it takes you six months to decide whether to proceed. So while you won't implement every idea that comes along, you should innovate frequently and rapidly.

While a major overhaul of a product line or business strategy should be approached with due prudence, implementing day-to-day innovations should be a streamlined process in your organization. No matter how strong the urge is to confirm your chances for success in advance, don't waste time writing and administering a research study. While such studies certainly have a place in your overall business strategy (see Lesson 37), the time it takes to write and administer them is a guaranteed momentum-killer. A well-conceived research study takes weeks or even months to execute. Meanwhile, so-called "intent-to-buy" studies—conventional alternative to the research study—are notoriously unreliable. Respondents who haven't personally used a product or service can scarcely assess their satisfaction with it, nor are they forking over their own hard-earned cash for a product—the ultimate test. Take the following advice to heart: the market will show whether or not an innovation is sound before a study ever will.

At Charlie Trotter's, energy is directed toward bringing an innovation to life and ensuring that it's given every chance to succeed—instead of trying to show why the company shouldn't take a chance on it. When Trotter or his staff have a good idea, he wastes no time implementing the innovation. Take the year he realized the kitchen would eventually need revamping. Some advisors suggested carrying out the renovation over a period of two years, spreading out the "down time" and the $750,000 in expenses. Trotter would have none of it. "Let's do it now," he said—and shut down the restaurant completely. Three weeks later, Trotter's cooks had a workstation commensurate with their skills and dedication: a rebuilt kitchen with the world's finest Bonnet ovens imported from France, state-of-the-art ventilation systems, space-saving work areas, and quick-clean floor and ceiling tiles.

Kicking Resistance: Stoking the Fire

Why are we slow to innovate? There's a simple answer: fear.

Maybe you remember past experiments that went awry, or worry about worst-case scenarios in the future. While only a fool refuses to learn from the past or plan for the future, most innovations are simply too incremental to bust your entire enterprise. Respect your past experience, but don't hang onto mistakes. Put failures behind you. Then accept that there's no way to know the future, even with the best projections. This philosophy will help you to overcome fear and act quickly.

Whatever you do, don't form committees to make decisions regarding innovations. Do it yourself. Because new ideas, products, and methods need to be consistent with your vision and standards, you need to determine whether innovations are right for your company. Moreover, you need to demonstrate decisiveness to employees if you expect them to have confidence in you as a leader. "For me, the problem with instant gratification is it takes too long," laughs Trotter. "If I decide to do something, I like to be able to do it immediately. A month for me is an eternity. I find that committee decision-making tends to be a lot slower than I want to go."

YOUR STAFF ISN'T GOING TO BOTHER TO PRESENT NEW IDEAS IF THOSE IDEAS ARE RARELY IMPLEMENTED—OR IF IT TAKES YOU SIX MONTHS TO DECIDE WHETHER TO PROCEED.

For the same reasons, don't hire outside consultants to determine whether an opportunity really exists or how to implement it. Consultants are trained to analyze, evaluate, calculate, and weigh the pros and cons—precisely the kinds of innovation-stifling activities you're trying to avoid. You know better than a consultant what will work for your company. So trust your intuition and take risks.

Before Trotter asks an idea generator to assess the human and capital resources his or her innovation would require, he has already decided it's an idea worth pursuing. To make sure innovations are developed and implemented quickly, Trotter sets tight deadlines of only a day or two for each step in the process. His innovator then assembles and leads a research-and-development team that will flash-test the innovation and bring it to life within two weeks.

Now matter what, eliminate forms and regulations. Every company has to maintain some amount of documentation, but forms and record-keeping chores bog down innovation. Wherever possible, dump requisition forms, reports, and paperwork. At the same time, encourage your staff to act and innovate, rather than report on what they plan to do or have already done. Employees who are forced to record the amount of time spent on every mundane task, mark down every step in their R&D process, or fill out a form every time they need simple supplies feel they're being treated like children and won't be easily motivated to innovate.

Free up your innovators so they can think and create. If you're a boutique owner, set a dollar limit, then let your window display artist buy the supplies she needs for her seasonal installations. If you're a software entrepreneur busy planning your company's expansion, allow your managers to approve unforeseen expenses that arise in the R&D process. If you're the publisher of a trade magazine planning to update its look, allow your designer to take a long lunch hour or report to work late to gather supplies or conduct research.

In the interest of both speed-to-market and employee motivation, it's sometimes necessary to hire people to temporarily or permanently replace idea-generating employees so they can concentrate on the innovation. After former manager Mark Signorio impressed Trotter with his innovative building design proposal, another employee was asked to assume 40 percent of Signorio's managerial responsibilities. In general, Trotter allows his most valuable and prolific innovators to spend ten to twenty hours a week working on their ideas. The freedom he's given them has paid off, showing that Trotter's discovered a winning recipe. He knows that the more space you give your innovators to develop, the more exciting ideas will flourish.

Ask Employees What Needs to Be Improved

"Men's faults do seldom make themselves appear," wrote William Shakespeare.

Besides creating an environment in which constant improvement is paramount, you need to be both brave and clear-sighted enough to pinpoint what's wrong and fix it. How to figure out which aspect of your business needs improvement first? Be prepared for it to come from sources you often overlook: your employees. To uncover some real answers about what needs to be improved, start by turning to the people in the trenches—those who spend as much time as you do at your business, and who can provide plenty of information about what needs to be improved.

Employees complain about the lousy photocopier, the location of cash registers, and the overwhelming number of customer service calls at a particular hour. The key is to ask employees what needs to be improved rather than wait for them to complain to you. Not only does the proactive approach help your company to deliver quality products and services, but also it convinces your staff how serious you are about customer satisfaction and that their ideas and contributions are important. What's more, if you and your employees don't routinely attempt to identify what needs to be improved, you can count on your customers taking their business someplace else.

As a rule of thumb, before heading out to inspect and analyze every method, employee, raw material, and piece of equipment associated with a customer concern, ask your employees in a departmentwide meeting. That way, you might be able to narrow the list of possible causes down to a handful before you start analyzing several processes and pieces of equipment. Ideally, if you and your staff can isolate trouble spots and take action, customers will find very little to complain about. To make sure staff members tell you what needs to be improved, you should do the following on a regular basis:

- **Tell your staff continuous improvement is essential to your vision.**

- **Ask employees how everyone in the company, including you, can improve.**

- **Every quarter, ask employees how they could improve themselves.**

- **Gather employees at least twice weekly to ask them what processes, products, and methods need to be improved.**

- **Make improvements based on their observations.**

- **Recognize and reward employees for their ideas.**

Particularly in successful businesses, it's vital that you persuade your staff to understand that continuous improvement is the only way you'll ever maintain excellence. To this end, you should stress the need to constantly improve so that it's ingrained in your staff's collective consciousness and they will be naturally inclined to strive to improve methods and procedures.

Provide examples of what happens to businesses that improve

and to those that don't. These instructive anecdotes should be clear and easy to understand. Take the case of Chrysler, which nearly went belly-up before it revamped its research and development, design, manufacturing processes, and marketing. Today, according to *U.S. News & World Report,* Chrysler's design team is considered the best in the world.

Demonstrate to employees how important continuous improvement is to you and your company by asking them to suggest—confidentially—in which areas you and the rest of the staff could improve. In a companywide meeting, distribute forms that ask staff to rate you and their fellow employees in regard to a variety of skills and functions, using a scale of 1 (needs major improvement) to 5 (needs very little improvement). Provide room for comments. If you have twenty-five employees, each staff member in the meeting should receive twenty-four forms to individually rate his or her colleagues on a range of criteria.

Employees can assess each other's cooperation, attention to detail, focus, determination, social skills, energy, efficiency, accuracy, professionalism, product knowledge, and work ethic. Assure your staff that absolutely no one will see the suggestions except the person for whom they're intended. Clearly, employees who receive 1s and 2s in a particular area from the majority of their peers know they really need to improve. Plus, it's a great way to encourage staff members to consider how they can improve themselves throughout the year.

In quarterly, private meetings, you should ask employees how they believe they could improve themselves. This shouldn't be an off-the-cuff discussion. You'll need to give it some thought before the meeting, so you can ask intelligent, targeted questions. Ask staff members individually: How would you rate your attention to detail? Determination? Social skills? Product knowledge? Work ethic? How could you improve your leadership skills? How could you be a better teammate? What could you do in order to make fewer mistakes?

What would make you a better cook, writer, salesperson, graphic artist, or publicist? In what areas do you feel you need the most improvement?

It's also smart to provide a regular time and place for employees to tell you what processes, products, and procedures need to be improved. Gather your staff a few times a week in a conference or meeting room for fifteen minutes to give them a chance to tell you what they think. Though they brainstorm at the daily preservice meeting, Charlie Trotter's staff also has the opportunity to tell management what methods, procedures, customer service approaches, and products need to be improved. Often, they have plenty to say without any prodding.

Your staff may know that customers feel service is too slow, for example, and the possible reasons why may be various. To elicit the details you need to take action, ask your staff pointed questions: Do you believe customer comments are justified? Why do you think we're slow? Do customer-service staff people have to wait on other departments before they can perform their jobs? What unnecessary procedures or methods can you identify? Which are necessary, but take too long to execute? Is a lack of tools or supplies preventing you from performing your job to the best of your ability? Which computers and other equipment cause you grief? Do you believe everyone is well trained to perform their work?

NOT ONLY DOES THE PROACTIVE APPROACH HELP YOUR COMPANY TO DELIVER QUALITY PRODUCTS AND SERVICES, BUT ALSO IT CONVINCES YOUR STAFF HOW SERIOUS YOU ARE ABOUT CUSTOMER SATISFACTION AND THAT THEIR IDEAS AND CONTRIBUTIONS ARE IMPORTANT.

Like Charlie Trotter and his managers, you should ask employees specific questions, such as: How could service have been better yesterday? Could our speed be improved? Could our response time be improved? Could we have better dazzled customers by our performance? How would you rate our product quality or selection? How could it be improved? Could our execution be improved? What kinds of problems did you notice? What customer complaints did you hear about products or service? Do you have the knowledge and resources to perform your job well?

Naturally, employees aren't always going to think of improvements during the meetings. That's why you also need to create a culture in which suggested improvements are welcomed and encouraged constantly. Instituting an "open door" policy is a good start. Basically, it's your job to remind staff members to come speak with you whenever they have a complaint or suggestion. When they take you up on your offer, put aside your work, don't take phone calls, don't allow other employees to interrupt your conversation, and don't be defensive.

Besides offering an open door, ask them what needs to be improved throughout the day, every day. Remember, many employees will be reluctant to make comments because they don't want to be considered whiners or know-it-alls, so it may take encouragement on your part. Observe them in the middle of work processes and ask them: Would you change the order of steps? Do you need better equipment or resources? What would allow you to perform your job faster? With more accuracy? With less waste? Whatever you do, make sure they know you appreciate their input by thanking them for their input, even when you don't plan to implement a change.

The best way to convince employees you appreciate their thoughts is to make frequent changes based on their input. This motivates them to speak up in the future, and it convinces them you're willing to put your money where your mouth is. Most important, never ignore valid complaints or tell employees you can't make improvements because you don't have the time to worry about it or you don't want to spend the money or because customers haven't complained yet. If you do, your staff will lose their belief in your commitment to excellence.

To really motivate employees to come forward with suggestions, recognize and reward them for their observations and suggestions. Improvements are just as important as innovations, so you should make it a matter of course to applaud your staff in front of the whole team. In your regular meetings, get excited about their ideas and schedule a time to look into each matter.

Squeamish about monetary recognition? Let's face it: some improvements save the company thousands of dollars or even save your entire business. You might also offer handsome pay increases to employees who regularly provide observations. Remember to note in the pay-raise envelope the reason why the employee is being rewarded. Bonuses need to be generous to have any significant motivational impact. Payouts equal to 5 percent of annual income are fairly generous.

Don't Be Afraid to Ask Customers What Needs to Be Improved,

Even If It Hurts

No matter how conscientious and unbiased you are when it comes to determining what needs to be improved in your business, the fact is you aren't objective. Maniacally vigilant as Charlie Trotter and his staff are, for example, they still miss things from time to time. They know they need to ask customers frequently and systematically what needs to be improved.

While this idea sounds easy to carry out, for many entrepreneurs, it's not. To put it bluntly, many of us fear that asking customers what needs to be improved is a tacit admission that our business is on the rocks and we're desperately begging for help from anyone who'll offer it. A pretty unpleasant image.

It's also a false one. The fact is that when you approach customers for their opinions, they're more often impressed by your self-confidence and your commitment to their satisfaction. Just try to recall the last time a restaurant, retailer, service organization, or corporation asked you to tell them how they could improve. Did you feel put off, or flattered?

Which customers should you approach? The answer is very simple: speak with anybody and everybody. You want to ask both first-time and regular customers; the young and old; male and female; native and foreign; in-state and out-of-state; affluent, middle- and low-income; educated and unschooled. However you go about it, be certain you don't just sample the opinions of friends and regular customers: they care about how you feel, and they're simply not as likely to be as forthright as new customers or travelers. Regulars, furthermore, are customers who are already sold on your business. You need to talk to people who aren't yet.

When to approach customers for their valuable opinions? A simple guideline: don't allow your desire to know what needs to be improved get in the way of customers' privacy and comfort. In other words, never call during the dinner hour, don't interrupt meetings or customer transactions, make sure you've given your customers sufficient time to experience the product or service, and ask questions only after they agree to speak with you. To a diner at a fine restaurant, for example, there's nothing more annoying than to be asked several questions seconds after being served a steaming and succulent entree. Let your customers get their business taken care of, so you can take care of yours.

To determine what aspects of your products need to be improved, ask willing customers: Could our product selection be improved? How? Could our product's durability, performance, appearance, comfort, style, taste, and reliability be improved? Are we innovative? Do our products have innovative features? Could product delivery be improved? In what respects? Are deliveries always correct, on time, and undamaged? Are the products you request always in stock? With which products have you had availability problems? Which products are inconsistent?

To glean intelligence on how your business's marketing could be improved, ask customers: Do we send an appropriate amount of marketing materials, such as fliers, newsletters, brochures, and postcards? Are our marketing materials, including advertisements, always of the highest quality? How could they be improved? Could our packaging be improved? How? Is it eye-catching? Could our product displays be improved? How? Are they overcrowded? Are products easy to reach? Are they attractive?

Because service is the aspect of your business that most personally affects customers, many will be delighted to talk with you about it. Ask them: Could employee product knowledge be improved? In what areas? Do employee communication skills need to be improved? How? Could employee attentiveness to your satisfaction and needs be improved? Do you ever have to wait to be approached by a sales or service person? At what times of day and for how long?

AT CHARLIE TROTTER'S EVERY EVENING, AS A MATTER OF COURSE, TROTTER AND STAFF SPEAK WITH CUSTOMERS BEFORE THEY'RE SEATED, DURING DINNER, AND AS THEY'RE LEAVING. THEY ASK NOT JUST THE CONVENTIONAL "IS EVERYTHING OK WITH YOUR MEAL?" BUT VERY SPECIFICALLY WHAT NEEDS TO BE CHANGED AND IMPROVED.

Do you ever have to ask for things more than once? How could the company better respond to your needs? Do employees always treat you with respect, courtesy, and kindness?

If you own a retail business, such as an art gallery, bookstore, or restaurant, it's also smart to ask customers how they feel about the physical space your business occupies. Could the design be improved? How? Is it too busy, too conservative, or too modern? Could the lighting or noise level be improved? How? The music selection? Is the temperature in the store comfortable? Which areas of the store are crowded? Could the store improve its accessibility?

In any business, cleanliness, tidiness, and organization are critical. Find out how your customers rate you by asking: Is our place of business always spotless from door to door? In which locations or areas have you noticed cleanliness problems? Could tidiness be improved? How? Do you find that we are one of the most organized companies you've ever experienced? Why or why not?

Now that you know who and what to ask, it's time to consider how to ask it. You have several options. Either approach customers individually for their input, assemble and moderate focus groups, or conduct simple questionnaires. At Charlie Trotter's every evening, as a matter of course, Trotter and staff speak with customers before they're seated, during dinner, and as they're leaving. They ask not just the conventional "Is everything OK with your meal?" but very specifically what needs to be changed and improved. Every customer in the restaurant, whether a fine-dining novice or a weekly customer, is fair game.

Steve Greystone is one of several customers whose perspective Trotter often seeks. "When I'm in the restaurant, he's always asking what I think of this or that, because he knows I notice and have an opinion. It's part of the fun," says Greystone. Without intruding for great lengths of time, Trotter or a dining room manager will inquire if Greystone finds the wine superior and the culinary creations not only sublime but balanced, heated, and prepared properly, as well as presented beautifully and served promptly. Trotter might even ask if the flowers are up to par, if the staff's level of enthusiasm is the best it can be, or if the room temperature is comfortable.

Focus Groups: Rounding up Customer Opinion

Assembling a focus group is a valuable way of gathering in-depth information when interviews are too difficult to administer due to the service delays or traffic problems they create. In the fast-food industry, for example, speed is the name of the game. Restaurant owners at these establishments can't take the time to interview customers about product quality and service. For businesses whose products are consumed off-site, customers can help assess service, but focus groups can be used to determine necessary product quality improvements.

To assemble an effective focus group that meets industry standards, you'll need to ask eight to twelve customers to come to your company or an off-site location during off-hours to discuss your company's products, marketing, service, physical space, and other details. As compensation for their time, it's best to give each participant complimentary products, gift certificates, or a $100 honorarium per one-hour session. In contrast to many other research subjects, focus group participants should be quite similar with respect to viewpoint and demographic makeup. In addition, it can be very valuable to invite people who aren't acquainted with one another and who've never participated in a focus group before. For Charlie Trotter's, it wouldn't make sense to assemble a group of regulars and novices, because the less-experienced camp would be uncomfortable and uncommunicative.

Rather than pay an expert through the nose, have yourself or one of your employees moderate the focus group discussion. Before the focus group convenes, prepare a list of areas you would like to address or prepare samples or prototype products for the group to evaluate. During the focus group, you should present these items for discussion, but allow the group to consider subjects raised by participants, too. The fact is, you might overlook a product characteristic, service component, or design element that a few individuals or the entire group consider to be extremely important. You'll be able to gain incredible insight, but be warned: eight or twelve opinions is by no means representative of all your customers or the general public.

Surveying the Crowd

Questionnaires provide another great opportunity to ask customers what needs to be improved. Provide respondents with a number of statements and ask if they agree or disagree with each. If your customers have bought a product or service, their answers should tell you which of your service staff waited on them, the date and time the respondent had a customer service interaction, and which product was purchased. You should also seek as many demographic details as possible about the customer, to determine if those factors affect customer response or satisfaction.

The following is an example of the one of the customer satisfaction surveys in use at Charlie Trotter's:

Charlie Trotter's Customer Satisfaction Survey

Please feel free to take this with you and return it at your convenience.

We value your impressions; please assist us in evaluating your dining experience.

Name _____ Date _____

Waiter _____ Table _____ Party _____

How did you hear about Charlie Trotter's? _____

Was this your first visit to Charlie Trotter's? ☐ Yes ☐ No

If not, when was the last time you were in? _____

Please answer the following questions on a scale of 1 to 5 where 3 is average, 1 is poor and 5 is outstanding. We also invite you to make any comments you feel appropriate.

Overall, how did you enjoy your evening? ____

Comment: _____

How would you rate the food? ____

Comment: _____

How would you rate the wine list? ____

Comment: _____

How would you rate your wait person? ____

Comment: _____

How would you rate the rest of the service staff? ____

Comment: _____

Do you plan to join us again in the future? ☐ Yes ☐ No

If no, please share your reason(s) with us:

_____

_____

What could we have done to improve your experience?

_____

_____

We would appreciate the following information in the event we need to contact you.

Name _____

Address _____

_____

Telephone _____

Thank you very much for your assistance.

A well-written and administered survey might indicate that service is not up to par or product quality is less than superior at certain hours of the day. Your job is to pinpoint the problem and make an improvement.

Finally, a word of caution: customers are one of the best instruments for measuring the success of your vision, but even the best barometers sometimes read wrong. In other words, despite the time-worn adage, the customer is not always right. At Charlie Trotter's, a multicourse degustation takes at least three hours to unfold and features artful presentations and preparations that require many steps. More important, the chef absolutely never allows food to be served that doesn't meet his expectations and specifications. For many customers, the lengthy experience is part of the pleasure. In other diners' minds, that's too long. But that doesn't mean the chef will speed up the evening to satisfy some customers. Like Trotter, you need to ask customers what needs to be improved, incorporate their opinion, yet ultimately, make decisions based on your vision.

Continually Improve Processes,

Upgrade Facilities, and Train Constantly

Today, the definitions of product and service excellence are continuously transforming. Consider the nonstop outpouring of safety and style enhancements in televisions, speed and memory upgrades in computers, or the advancements in international parcel deliveries. Definitions of product and service excellence are always changing and transforming.

Charlie Trotter knows this well. You might think that in 1998, after his restaurant was named the best in the world by the readers of

Wine Spectator for the second straight year, Trotter would kick back and take it easy for a while. Not a chance. Says the chef: "All excellent businesses are driven by the idea they're going to be improved constantly." Their credo? "Nothing is ever good enough. Never grow satisfied or complacent, never take anything for granted."

Is Trotter simply a fanatic, unable to sit back and enjoy his accomplishments? Successful business analysts like Steve Greystone don't think so. "Charlie Trotter understands what he's accomplished is on a high level, so he's pleased to some extent with his success, but never really happy," notes Greystone, who's observed the chef on dozens of occasions. "When Trotter gets news that he's been granted some award or great honor, invariably, his first response is, 'OK. Now we've got to get better.' The fact is, he's right. After winning, there's more scrutiny and a higher expectation level. When it comes to top-level restaurants that are considered great, as a customer, you expect a lot—sometimes more than can be delivered. It's like going to see Pavarotti at the opera. You're expecting his voice to be in great shape and determined for it to be one of the great experiences of your life."

Trotter strives to meet those standards of perfection. He knows the restaurant's employees, methods, marketing, product quality, and customer service have to continuously improve, because what's excellent today isn't necessarily going to be considered excellent tomorrow. The same will be true in your own business.

Occasionally, an entrepreneur comes along who is damn near obsessed with making improvements. As a pioneer of East Coast health maintenance organizations for two decades, Patient InfoSystems CEO Don Carlberg witnessed managed health care's greatest advances and its most daunting and costly problems. Why, for example, were some HMO patients clearly improving and others not, in groups with identical diagnoses and prescriptions? "Traditionally," says Carlberg, "we blamed the doctors." Yet when push came to shove, medical analysts could find no evidence of faulty treatment.

Visionary Carlberg was one of the first in the HMO industry to look beyond the physicians in analyzing the source of the problem, and statistics would eventually bear out his hunch, showing that between 30 to 60 percent of all patients actually fail to adhere to prescribed treatment plans. In 1995, Carlberg began building an entire company around this "missing link" between doctors' orders and good health. Reading industry literature, the health care entrepreneur came across information on the remarkable effectiveness of computerized disease management programs, including patient reminder calls, in improving patient health. Even more surprising, studies showed that patients respond more truthfully when speaking to a computer than to a live human being when discussing sensitive health-related subjects such as sexual behavior and emotional matters. His readings gave Carlberg an idea: he would combine automated interviewing programs with basic technology present in 90 percent of all American homes—the telephone—to gather important information for health providers. Three years after he began, Carlberg's cutting-edge company, Patient InfoSystems, has gone public, is tripling its facilities, and is greatly expanding its client base.

Observe, Evaluate, and Improve

To identify shortcomings in the way your business performs, you need to enlist the help of your front-line troops who are "in the trenches" day in and day out. Meet with employees who perform each particular task and ask them to detail every single step involved in their work flow. Then write down all the steps in the order they're performed. (With this list in hand, it's much easier to keep in mind the nuances of the operation and analyze it later.) Next, watch your employees perform each task and see if you can recommend changes. Also ask staff members carrying out each job if they can think of a new or better method, layout, or order of tasks to get the job done.

Let's consider a given project—say, a mass advertising mailing.

The project involves folding materials and stuffing, sealing, labeling, and posting envelopes. Simple? Only if you're not paying attention to detail. Believe it or not, there are several possible ways to perform each function—countless variations on how to stack and position the materials, several methods for stuffing, labeling, and so on. You and your staff need to figure out the most efficient order, technique, and layout of employees and materials.

Now it's time to evaluate how to improve and/or update equipment. Make a list of these items, then ask the employees who use each one to tell you which should be evaluated first. Take their suggestions and consult the manufacturer's instructions, marketing materials, and warranty to determine how each product or piece of equipment is supposed to be used and how it is expected to respond or perform. If a piece of equipment does what it's supposed to do but it just doesn't meet your needs or standards, it's time to upgrade.

Once you identify an equipment problem, it's time to implement changes and evaluate the results. Make changes on a limited basis at first, compare the new outcomes with the present status quo, and then determine if the changes should be made companywide. To ensure that your evaluation is accurate, hold all the other factors constant. At Charlie Trotter's, for example, the chef and his cooks might believe using a particular brand of sauté pan is the reason that certain sauces burn easily. Before buying several new pans, the restaurant first experiments with a variety of pans to determine if the equip-

> "WHEN TROTTER GETS NEWS THAT HE'S BEEN GRANTED SOME AWARD OR GREAT HONOR, INVARIABLY, HIS FIRST RESPONSE IS, 'OK. NOW WE'VE GOT TO GET BETTER.'"
>
> — Steve Greystone, longtime Trotter's customer

ment is really the source of the problem. The cook selects and measures identical sets of ingredients, uses the old and new pans side by side over the same heat setting, and then cooks the sauce for the same length of time in each. If Trotter and his cooks are confident that the sauce turns out better in a particular pan, the restaurant might order the product or experiment with other alternatives until they find what they need.

There is another very important aspect of your business that will always need improving: the people. Both you and your employees operate equipment, perform steps in processes, use a variety of methods, and select and use raw materials. Identify the individuals who are involved in processes, products, and service areas that are flagged for improvement and supervise them carefully performing each method and using equipment; identify those individuals who need improvement.

If an employee performs certain functions slowly or inefficiently, or doesn't use equipment as well as possible, or is a poor judge of which materials to use, you or one of your managers need to spot the problem and retrain them on the spot. If they're using the materials or equipment properly and it still doesn't perform to the manufacturer's description, call the dealer.

The quest never ends. Trotter is always searching for ways to improve processes, people, raw materials, and equipment, even when customers and employees don't perceive a problem or need for improvement. Even though the reviews say the foodstuffs used at Trotter's couldn't be any better, for example, the chef-owner routinely seeks a better supplier of produce, seafood, or meats whose products eclipse anything customers have ever sampled.

To find the best raw materials and equipment, you must constantly evaluate every product you can get your hands on; read religiously to learn about developments in your industry; travel, shop, and search in out-of-state and foreign markets; tell vendors you're willing to pay for the best; and ask peers for recommendations. Indeed, when you are willing to change vendors regularly to ensure the best possible quality, they are highly motivated to continuously improve in order to keep you as a client.

Reinvest in Your Business,

or What to Do with All the Money

You're Going to Make

Many books about small business management include a lot of information about business plans, financial statements, profit-and-loss statements, bookkeeping records, and taxes. Some even include complicated formulas, regulations, sample ledgers, and worksheets. And for good reason: many entrepreneurs, from novices to seasoned veterans, find accounting both boring and mind-boggling. Yet every year, even excellent, profitable small businesses fail due to poor money management.

Though Charlie Trotter is a savvy businessperson, like most entrepreneurs he pays an accountant to manage his company's accounts and finances. Trotter knows that no matter how small your business is, it's a good idea to hire a qualified CPA. Most hard-working entrepreneurs don't have the time, training, or know-how to successfully manage a company's accounting. Conversely, CPAs are well versed in all matters legal and financial; the bottom line is that their expertise will add money to your bank account in the long run.

After you pay an accountant to calculate exactly how much money your company has earned each month and year, you need to do something productive with the loot. Like Charlie Trotter, you should reinvest in your company (with an average yearly growth of 20 percent, Trotter's has found reinvestment to be a wise idea indeed). Simply put, your ultimate goal should be to use the money to increase profitability (decrease costs and increase revenues).

To reinvest in your company and boost profits, pay your employees industry-leading salaries. This is one investment guaranteed to pay dividends. Well-paid staff members will remain with you for years and become increasingly efficient. Indeed, an $80,000 salaried employee with ten years' experience, knowledge, and training will be able to do the work of two new hires brought in at $60,000. Consider all that you invest in each employee: first you spend a great deal of time and energy hiring the best people, then you spend months or years indoctrinating, training, teaching, motivating, and supervising them. Employee turnover creates tons of costly hidden expenses and therefore erodes profits.

Without doubt, Charlie Trotter's employees earn some of the highest incomes in the U.S. restaurant community. Though the entire staff is well compensated, several senior managers earn six-figure incomes and cooks earn more than most of their peers. Heed Trotter's advice: excellent employees are difficult and costly to replace, so it's critical you continue to invest in your staff.

To find out what a top salary is, you'll need to do some homework. Many industry trade magazines, such as *Restaurants and Institutions,* and news magazines, including *U.S. News & World Report,* report leading and average salaries by job title. Additionally, you can call competitors and interview employees from other companies to determine leading salaries for specific job titles.

No matter how good your benefits package is, your goal should be to offer the best package under the sun. Say you already offer a 401(k) plan, fully paid health and dental insurance, life insurance, profit sharing, and leaves of absence. If you now match 50 percent of employee 401(k) contributions, gradually increase the match to 75 percent, and then 100 percent, and so on. Furthermore, you should become increasingly generous as profits increase.

Continuously invest in employee training, equipment, and supplies, to improve not only quality, but efficiency and productivity as well. Buy well-made, labor- and space-saving equipment that allows you to conserve labor and reduce waste and computerware that helps to eliminate errors. Charlie Trotter invested $750,000 in the restaurant's kitchen for its remodel, equipping it with easy-to-clean and easy-to-maintain surfaces and tiles, space-saving counters and cabinets, and the most energy-efficient, long-lasting, accurate Bonnet ovens. When better equipment comes along, he'll upgrade again.

Charlie Trotter's constantly updates and renovates its facilities to deliver excellence and satisfy customers. Particularly if you're in the retail business or client services, it's important to frequently redecorate and renovate your store, offices, restaurant, or club. The key is to change before it's time to change. Buy beautiful flower arrangements, fine artwork, area rugs, lighting fixtures, and the like to decorate your store or offices. Paint and wallpaper and replace the carpet every two or three years.

Clearly, marketing is the key to driving your business. That's why you need to invest the money to continuously upgrade marketing materials and your database management system. Take some of your earnings and invest them in the best professional photography, custom illustrations, and sophisticated computer design programs and graphics to enrich your marketing materials. You also need to invest in your database system regularly to make sure the names and addresses are accurate and easy to reference.

A relatively common way to reinvest in a business is to expand or relocate. To continue to grow, you may need additional space to serve customers or manufacture goods, a completely new look, or better access to public transportation. You might even want a prestigious address after you grow significantly. Many advertising and public relations agencies in New York City, for example, are located on Madison Avenue, the famous district synonymous with success. For advertising firms, having an address there can mean the difference between a lucrative contract and a lukewarm one.

Charlie Trotter built a new dining room addition onto his restaurant several years ago. Sure it cost a bundle, but over the years Trotter's has been able to seat as many as seventy additional customers every night (at $135 per person, you do the math). He also added a "studio" kitchen and small dining room in the converted town house next door to handle consulting engagements and large corporate parties. In fact, the demo kitchen is the set for Trotter's PBS series, which helps to publicize and market his cooking and restaurant, too.

HEED TROTTER'S ADVICE: EXCELLENT EMPLOYEES ARE DIFFICULT AND COSTLY TO REPLACE, SO IT'S CRITICAL YOU CONTINUE TO INVEST IN YOUR STAFF.

Some entrepreneurs open additional locations as a way to reinvest in their businesses. The problem is that quality often suffers at one or all of the outlets, because the leader and motivator cannot be everywhere at once. Not to mention that earning a profit at the new location isn't necessarily going to allow for reinvestment in the core business, unless enough money is made to split the profits between two entities.

Charlie Trotter has discovered that a great way to reinvest in his core business and enhance his marketing at the same time is to develop product-line extensions and market new products. By investing restaurant profits toward the publishing of cookbooks, marketing retail gourmet sauces, and producing educational videos, he earns supplemental income for the restaurant and promotes the Charlie Trotter's brand to gourmets nationally. You could consider adding new products to your line, selling your products through different channels, or offering services on-line.

Charlie Trotter never stops looking for ways to improve his business. It's no wonder all aspects of it continue to get better and better. What's interesting is that increasing his short-term improvement costs in many areas of his business has proven to lead to increased profitability in the long run. The reason? The costs he incurs make his business increasingly efficient, eliminating greater costs he would incur over time.

excellence

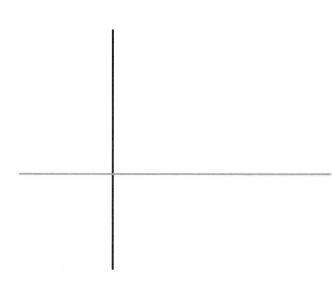

AND YOUR PUBLIC

34 Touch Your Customers

(Figuratively, of Course)

Small businesses are forever hunting for ways to distinguish themselves from the competition. They begin with a creative name, then stock new product lines, redesign their facilities, buy their employees new uniforms, offer frequent promotions, or distribute "preferred customer" cards. These surface touches are lovely—but not always effective.

A surefire way to separate yourself from the crowd is to touch your customers with kind, thoughtful gestures as often as possible. Your actions should demonstrate you really care about them, and thereby instill a feeling of loyalty in your patrons towards your business and its place in the community.

Think of the last time a waiter at an establishment you patronize remembered that you prefer your house salad with vinaigrette on the side, extra fresh ground pepper, and no raw onions. "I can't believe she remembered that," you surely thought to yourself. How did this simple act make you feel? Appreciated, touched? Even important? These are the kinds of feelings you want to evoke in your customers on a regular basis.

Unfortunately, many small businesses simply don't bother to provide the personal touches that help to turn great businesses into excellent enterprises. The reasons? Either entrepreneurs don't know they should, think they don't have the time, or feel they don't have the money.

Everyone is different and has different life experiences, so what touches one person might not affect another. That's why you and your employees need to communicate with your customers on the phone and in person, day in and day out. Ask customers simple questions, such as: Did you enjoy your weekend? Did you have a nice holiday? How is your work lately? How is your retirement or summer vacation treating you? What are your plans for the summer? What did you think of the NBA Finals? You never know what kinds of information you'll learn. Maybe you'll discover one customer bought a new summer home, a regular guest lost a loved one, another gave birth to a child, and someone else is about to embark on a trip to the Far East. The key is to use the information in the future to touch customers.

Small gestures can make an enormous difference. Last year, the three-year-old son of this book's author was severely burned in a kitchen accident at home. Since that time, owners and employees at two local businesses have regularly asked how the child is faring and if his skin is recovering. Their simple acts of thoughtful kindness are genuinely touching and certainly make their overall customer service superior. At Charlie Trotter's, a customer who is sick might receive a special delivery from the restaurant. A guest who just returned from Asia might be treated to a special regional delicacy to remind him of his trip.

Like the server or bartender who remembers your favorite beverage, you need to remember and even note your customers' preferences so you can truly take care of them. For starters, keep computer files on your customers to note the quantities they usually order; the product types, brands, colors, patterns, styles, and flavors they prefer; how they like products to be made or prepared; the way they like their goods to be packaged and shipped; where they like products to be delivered; their usual method of payment; and special requests. Most important, use the information to dazzle your guests.

"When a guest has dined with us before," says Judi Carle of Charlie Trotter's, "we have a better idea of what will send them 'over the edge.' We have one customer, for example, whom we know loves both the butter we use and our smoked salmon. As he's leaving, we've given him a gift bag containing a pound of butter and a package of salmon. The gesture costs very little, and lets our guest know we think he's special."

Most of us appreciate when friends and family members remember our birthdays and wedding anniversaries or recognize work promotions or recent graduations. When was the last time a small business remembered your birthday? Want to go a step further? Most customers are delighted to receive complimentary items. On special occasions, it's worth your while to do so. Thanks to your ongoing communication with customers, you should be able to tailor gifts to individual tastes. To provide a special touch, give loyal customers boxes of chocolates, magazine subscriptions, bottles of wine, best-selling books, compact discs, or tickets to theater and sporting events. At Charlie Trotter's, it's not uncommon for the chef to send a gratis course of food or a bottle of champagne to a regular customer. Other customers might receive an autographed copy of one of his books or a guided tour of the facilities. Even first-time diners enjoy complimentary *amuse-gueule* and petits fours.

Another highly effective way to make customers feel special is to devise regular customer service perks that are creative, uncommon, and distinctive. Take the example set by the Sunset Foods staff in Northbrook, Illinois. As standard service, the market's employees offer customers a complimentary, freshly brewed cup of coffee, unload every customer's groceries onto the checkout conveyors, and even load groceries into cars. Some other ideas? Hold the door open for all your customers, offer hors d'oeuvres or glasses of champagne in your retail business, or hire a musician to entertain guests or shoppers. Or as Chicago's Bella Vista restaurant has done, include a car wash with your valet service.

Charlie Trotter personally goes to great lengths to touch customers with exceptional service. On special occasions, the chef himself has picked up out-of-town guests from O'Hare airport, a good twenty miles away from the restaurant. He's delivered Charlie Trotter's "takeout" to ill customers and prepared and served elaborate dinners in customers' homes.

You can provide a superb touch by delivering unanticipated quality and elegance in specific areas. Packaging materials, for example, should be made of quality and even recyclable materials and be sturdy, durable, attractive, easy to read, and possibly reusable. Payard Cafe and Patisserie in New York City, for example, uses lovely boxes to package baked goods, convincing customers in advance of the high quality and attention to detail in every aspect of the operation.

Intent on touching customers in every way possible, Charlie Trotter's is committed to serving food and wine with china and glassware fit for royalty. The restaurant uses an unprecedented variety of Riedel stemware, considered by many wine aficionados to be hands-down superior. Meals arrive at the table on

AT CHARLIE TROTTER'S, IT'S NOT UNCOMMON FOR THE CHEF TO SEND A GRATIS COURSE OF FOOD OR A BOTTLE OF CHAMPAGNE TO A REGULAR CUSTOMER. OTHER CUSTOMERS MIGHT RECEIVE AN AUTOGRAPHED COPY OF ONE OF HIS BOOKS OR A GUIDED TOUR OF THE FACILITIES. EVEN FIRST-TIME DINERS ENJOY COMPLIMENTARY **AMUSE-GUEULE** AND PETITS FOURS.

some of the finest china in the world, from Great Britain's Wedgwood to France's Bernardaud Limoges. As if that isn't enough, the restaurant adds *la crème de la crème* by serving every course on a different china pattern.

"The china at Charlie Trotter's illustrates the attention to detail," says WLS-TV Chicago news anchor and customer Linda Yu. "Those are the very special touches of someone who has thought through every single thing. It would be easy to buy or design Charlie Trotter's china. But what a fabulous touch that every course comes on something different." Indeed, while other four-star fine-dining restaurants use fine china rather than commercial-grade plateware, none stock so many different patterns.

You also need to touch your customers by doing and providing the unexpected. To open the doors for customers or serve champagne to guests at Tiffany might not seem remarkable. But to provide table service at your fast-food restaurant or complimentary gourmet coffee at your local service station might be just the kind of touch that will separate your business as one of the best. Ask yourself: What could we do that customers would never in their wildest dreams expect? What services could we perform that no other businesses in our community or industry offer? What special amenities could we offer that would sweep customers off their feet?

Touch customers on a regular basis and you will occupy a very special place in their minds. Your customers will repay you with loyalty and referrals. What better way to evoke strong, positive feelings than to make sure customers haven't a care in the world when they patronize your establishment or conduct business with you? You and your employees need to be highly attentive and anticipate your customers' needs. When it's raining and you notice a customer has forgotten her umbrella, run and get her car. These simple touches will send your business over the top.

Pick Your Customers

or They'll Pick You

To be able to buy the best materials, invest in training, reward your people, offer good benefits, and upgrade equipment frequently, you're going to need a large customer base generating plenty of sales revenue. And it takes a lot more than superior products and tremendous service to achieve that goal.

Charlie Trotter knows this, and he pursues the kind of revenue-generating ventures needed to position his business as a dominant force in the marketplace. He frequently appears on the radio and TV and gives speeches at conferences and business schools several times a year to build his consulting business. His company has to sell private parties; market special events, products, and cookbooks; and publicize itself to generate the cash flow necessary to enable it to create superior products and offer tremendous service in the first place.

Though his products and books appeal to relatively diverse audiences, Charlie Trotter believes his company's core product—the four-star dining experience—is most suited for a very specific type of customer. Charlie Trotter's restaurant targets customers who are serious devotees of food and wine. As a group, they read culinary magazines, collect rare vintage wines, and dine out frequently, both locally and internationally. What's more, the majority are well-educated professionals and senior managers. Trotter's average diner is in his forties, affluent, well-traveled, a resident of one of the world's large cosmopolitan cities, and a connoisseur of the finer things in life. To a lesser extent, the restaurant markets to a broader group of consumers that can afford the restaurant for very special occasions but are perhaps not as food knowledgeable, affluent, or traveled as the primary target.

You, too, must carefully pick an appropriate target market by identifying the group of consumers that is most likely to respond favorably to the distinguishing characteristics and strengths of your products or services. The target group you identify needs to be large enough to provide enough sales to keep your business viable, yet homogenous enough so that your firm can bring each customer exceptional satisfaction. If your enterprise offers a range of products, you may need to identify more than one target market.

Before you start segmenting your target, bear in mind that population subgroups are never entirely homogenous. Take the age group of twenty-five to thirty-four, for example. Clearly a twenty-eight-year-old attorney earns more than a twenty-eight-year-old clerical worker and has a different level of education and probably a different lifestyle. And many marketers would argue that a twenty-five-year-old is not much like a thirty-four-year-old (and even other twenty-five-year-olds) when it comes to lifestyle and social opinions. That's why you need to target consumers using several specific characteristics.

There are a variety of ways to segment markets. Take out a piece of paper and pencil—it's time to write down some key information about your business's consumers. You can distinguish markets based on the following characteristics:

- **Demographics (income, gender, age, occupation, family size, education, race, and social class)**

- **Psychographics (activities, interests, and opinions)**

- **Purchasing behavior or rate of use**

- **Geographical location**

- **Needs (economic, psychological, physiological, and social)**

Demographics remain the most common basis for segmentation. You'll need to consider income, sex, age, occupation, family size, education, race, and social class to determine which demographic market segments will respond most favorably to your products or service. Ask yourself: What income level responds most favorably to our product? Do mostly males or females buy or use our products or services? What advantage would we gain from targeting one sex rather than the other? What age group responds most favorably to our product? What age groups ought to respond more favorably?

What specific professionals or occupations respond most favorably to our product? Do large, medium, or small families respond most favorably to our product? Do singles use our products? What advantage would we gain from targeting one family size rather than another? What level of education responds most favorably to our product? What advantage would we gain from targeting consumers according to their education level? Do our products appeal more to one race than another? Which social classes respond most favorably to our product? Which social classes should be attracted to our products?

Psychographics (also known as lifestyle analysis) segment consumers according to their activities, interests, and opinions. Activities include hobbies, entertainment, club membership, and athletic endeavors. Interests such as fashion, music, and food are factored into psychographic analysis, as are political and cultural opinions. To segment according to psychographics, ask yourself: Do our customers perform or take part in certain activities more than others? Which activities? Are our customers likely to have certain hobbies? Which hobbies? Are they gourmet cooks, theater buffs, club members, bowlers, or cyclists? Are our customers food or fashion lovers? Do our customers have unique interests? What advantage would we gain from targeting consumers according to their lifestyle? Are our customers socially and/or fiscally conservative or liberal?

It's smart to segment according to purchasing behavior or rate of use, too, and then combine this information with demographic and psychographic information. Ask yourself questions such as: What rate is considered heavy use of our product or service? (Heavy use of Charlie Trotter's restaurant might be once a month, for example.) Who are our heavy users? What is their age, income, sex, occupation, etc.? What kinds of lifestyles do they have? After you develop a demographic profile of heavy users, you market to nonusers who have the same demographic characteristics.

Segmenting according to geographical location is another useful step in target marketing. Depending on the nature and scope of your business, you could segment suburbs, U.S. cities, states, regions, zip codes (10021, 60093, and 90210, for example, are affluent neighborhoods), and regions of the world. Charlie Trotter's markets itself not only locally, but also nationally and internationally, because the restaurant depends upon business and leisure travelers to fill the seats five nights a week. Thanks to census data and lifestyle data from companies such as Claritas and Donnelley Marketing Information Services, it's possible to target working-class, middle-class, or affluent areas; areas with a high proportion of seniors; or areas with a great number of evangelical Christians. Each of these groups represents a different potential target market.

Your marketing can also be based on customer needs or need-driven behavior. Consider: What needs do our products fulfill? Do

THE TARGET GROUP YOU IDENTIFY NEEDS TO BE LARGE ENOUGH TO PROVIDE ENOUGH SALES TO KEEP YOUR BUSINESS VIABLE, YET HOMOGENOUS ENOUGH SO THAT YOUR FIRM CAN BRING EACH CUSTOMER EXCEPTIONAL SATISFACTION.

our products provide economic security? Do our products provide value? Do our products make customers feel good about themselves? Do our products save customers time? Do our products provide status? Are our products healthful? Do they enhance beauty? Then ask yourself what kinds of customers have these needs and target them.

After you write down the answers to all these questions, develop a profile or composite sketch of your target customers. Remember, you are going to tailor your marketing campaign and message to a target group that is fairly homogenous. After you figure out who is right for your product or products, you'll decide whether to use public relations, advertising, direct mail, sales, or promotion (or any combination of them) to convey your marketing message to various groups of consumers.

Don't Be Afraid to
Fire Customers

After you pick your customers by carefully targeting a relatively homogenous market, it's time to narrow that market further. More than likely, some customers aren't right for your business, particularly if yours is an enterprise that attempts to offer customers truly distinctive products or services. So get rid of the customers who aren't right. This contemporary and somewhat unconventional business practice is known as "firing customers."

"If you want to make your business better sometimes, it's not always a question of trying to make every customer happy," explains Trotter. "Maybe it's better to fire certain segments of your customer base to make what you do even better for your best customers.

"Over the years we have done a number of things to fire customers, and I'm not hesitant at all," admits Trotter. "It's not that I don't appreciate our customers, but sometimes it's better for me to take care of those who really understand this type of dining and not to worry about trying to satisfy everybody. We have deliberately, definitively cut off more and more segments of our customer base."

Why would any business want to get rid of paying customers? For one thing, your product, company, or service is defined not only by its features, uses, and benefits, but also by its customers or users. Also, in service businesses, certain customers—for example, smokers or young children—could alienate your best customers. Most important, the objective of firing is not simply to get rid of certain customers, but to fine-tune the product or the marketing message for your target market.

It may sound cold and harsh, but it's an essential step in positioning your business in the marketplace: take deliberate steps to alienate certain customers and focus your attention on your best customers (defined by rate of purchase or sales volume, for example) or the customers you are best able to serve. Still sounds risky, doesn't it? Don't worry, most businesses can afford to lose certain customers, so long as you improve your product positioning, gain new customers, and build loyalty among your client base.

For starters, you need to examine your product positioning and your target customers. Positioning is an effort to fit a product or service to a market to set it apart from the competition. To ensure a good fit, your product or service might need to be altered, the market you serve might need to be changed, and the marketing message might need to be tweaked. To get the ball rolling there are some questions you'll want to ask yourself: What position does my product or service occupy in my target customer's mind? How is it positioned? By product, price, quality, the way it's used, or by the type of user? How well does it fit the market? How could I better position it? How many of my customers can I afford to lose to better satisfy a more precisely targeted market? If my aim is to distinguish my business from the competition, are there enough customers to fit that niche?

More than likely, your product could be better or at least differently positioned, and there are probably ways to better distinguish yourself from the competition. Perhaps your company strictly makes high-quality running shoes, but you've discovered that many customers are buying the shoes for walking and hiking. You could, of course, simply take their money and not question their erroneous understanding of your product. However, if you happen to have the competitive edge in the running-shoe market—because you hired the best engineers and designers—and want your company to be known as the best running-shoe manufacturer in the nation, you may not want the shoes you manufacture to be perceived as all-purpose or cross-training footwear.

What to do? You guessed it. It's time to fire some customers. To do so, you've got a number of different options, from the subtle to the more flagrant. Change is the key word. Charge a premium price and change your advertising to reflect the types of people who wear the shoes: serious runners who race, run year-round, or believe walking is for wimps. Change product features, name, image. If it's not clear from the shoe design what type of shoe it is, the packaging or point-of-purchase merchandising might better reflect this as a high-performance running shoe. Change your packaging. Change your advertising message to emphasize different benefits or rewards. Market yourself through new and different media outlets.

If yours is a service business, change hours of operation, dress codes, or overall ambiance. Create or change company policies: an advertising agency could choose to represent only luxury goods manufacturers and thereby fire all mass-market goods manufacturers, for example. A shopping mall could choose to include certain stores to create an image and alter its client base.

The objective is to create a product or service that is most appealing to a highly targeted market. In the aforementioned examples, the running-shoe manufacturer, advertising agency, and shopping mall would lose a certain number of clients. But the result is a very clear positioning in the target consumer's mind as to what the company or product represents and what kinds of customers it attracts. As a result, the company is more likely to attract the kinds of customers it desires and can hope to generate the most revenue.

To consider which customers to alienate, it's also helpful to revisit segmenting characteristics—demographic, psychographic, geographic, and need-based segmenting characteristics. You can further narrow the target market by reconsidering the segmenting characteristics and how changes in policy or concept would lead to firing certain segments. To fire according to income, you might change the price of your product, for example. To fire according to geographic location, you might offer local residents a discount.

Say you are the owner of a jazz club in a major city, such as New York, San Francisco, or Chicago. For the most part, your target customers are local urbanites who enjoy jazz music, but you want to better position your establishment so it's not perceived as just another nightclub. You could further segment the market by charging $10 admission (which would target specific income and age groups), enforcing a black-tie dress code (target income and social class), and offering only big-band jazz (target specific interests).

In other words, you could position your club as the place for well-heeled, sharp-dressed, big-band jazz lovers. Simultaneously, you would fire anyone who likes other forms of jazz music, such as fusion or bebop, cannot afford or refuses to pay the admission, and doesn't own a tuxedo or evening gown or would rather not dress so formally to listen to jazz music.

Charlie Trotter's target customers love fine food and wine, read food and wine publications, religiously collect rare wines, have hefty incomes, are willing to spend over $100 per person to dine in a fine restaurant, dine out frequently, travel internationally, are urban, and are aged in their forties. This somewhat homogenous target group, however, allows for lots of variation.

Some diners who fit the broad target market love red meat, while others are vegetarian. Plenty of diners who are well-heeled are not crazy about seafood or game meats. Many fine-dining lovers, affluent or not, are accustomed to eating an appetizer or salad, entree, and dessert. A fair number prefer large portions and expect to dine in less than two hours. Some diners still smoke. And most everyone is accustomed to choosing what they want to eat from a menu.

Because there is too much variation in the target market, Trotter decided to further segment and narrow the market after the restaurant had been in business for a few years. He believed there was a core group of customers he could satisfy better than any other restau-

"IT'S NOT THAT I DON'T APPRECIATE OUR CUSTOMERS, BUT SOMETIMES IT'S BETTER FOR ME TO TAKE CARE OF THOSE WHO REALLY UNDERSTAND THIS TYPE OF DINING AND NOT WORRY ABOUT TRYING TO SATISFY EVERYBODY. WE HAVE DELIBERATELY, DEFINITIVELY CUT OFF MORE AND MORE SEGMENTS OF OUR CUSTOMER BASE."

— Charlie Trotter

rant in the city, but to truly satisfy this highly targeted group would require alienating other customers. And that's OK.

Trotter narrowed his target market with a seating policy (on Friday and Saturday the restaurant seats every fifteen minutes from 5:30 to 6:30 p.m. and from 8:30 to 10 p.m.), fixed-price multicourse dining format, nonsmoking environment, predominantly healthful menu items, sparing use of red meat, and a vegetarian tasting menu, among other things. Finicky eaters, pretheater diners, smokers, red meat lovers, and vegetable haters probably do not dine frequently at Charlie Trotter's, but the restaurant better satisfies its target customers.

Restaurant reviewer Phil Vettel of the *Chicago Tribune* believes Trotter is one of only a handful of chefs who have dared to fire customers. "Diners wanted to come to restaurants and have a couple of appetizers and bolt. 'Hey, that's fine.' Jackets and ties? 'Don't worry about it.' 'Sure, we've got a booster seat if you want to bring your ill-mannered child along.' The economy got tighter and competition got tougher, so restaurateurs found it difficult to say 'no' to anybody. Charlie is occasionally at least willing to say 'no.' In fact," says Vettel, "he has set the kinds of standards such that certain questions don't even get asked."

excellence

IN MARKETING,

PUBLICITY, AND

SALES

Determine the Information Needed

Before Conducting Market Research

When Charlie Trotter attended college, studying philosophy and political science, he had no intention of becoming a gourmet chef or celebrity restaurateur. Five years later, having changed his focus 180 degrees and opened his fine-food eatery, it never occurred to Trotter that his political science background would be an asset. Bygone days of calculating demographics, public trends, and opinions, he thought, were over. But entrepreneurs like Trotter—and you—are constantly faced with difficult and important marketing decisions to make—and these factors are fundamental to the strategic positioning of your business in the marketplace. Day after day, you have to learn as much as possible about consumer needs and desires. Based on the data you collect and the conclusions you draw, you'll introduce products, kill products, change product features, promote products differently, market to new audiences, sell through different channels, and change prices to ensure the marketing mix fits the target market.

Marketing research—including focus groups, research studies, and observation—provides decision-makers like you with the information required to make these strategic decisions involving the company's future and evaluate structures that are already in place.

When you design a study, you'll gather demographic, geographic, and lifestyle information along with information regarding your marketing mix in order to cross-tabulate customer profiles with responses. Why must you group responses demographically? Let's face it: wealthy corporate executives probably will respond differently than college students to a study investigating reaction to prices, and you will need to consider the disparity when evaluating the data.

What Are You Looking For?

The first step in the marketing research process is to define why you want the information. Is it to find out what your customer base is? To determine what will make your clients happy? So that you can plan future business strategy? Such considerations may sound obvious, but many marketing research studies are undertaken before anyone determines precisely what it is they want to learn!

It's vital to have the research objectives clearly defined. Should the firm know more about how the local economy affects consumers and the business community? How the national economy affects consumers and the business community? About the public's understanding of the economy? How do interest rate fluctuations affect business? How does overall inflation affect your industry or business in general? How does a bull or bear market affect consumer decision making?

With respect to the political environment, ask yourself: Does our firm need to better understand how policy changes affect consumer attitudes and demand? Do we need to know how consumers in general view government or the political process? Whether our community is mostly Republican or Democrat? Whether our community or the nation is politically active? Whether or not people in our community vote?

When it comes to the cultural and social environment, ask yourself: What kind of values does the public hold today? What are the most popular styles of music today? What books and magazines are consumers reading? What are the community's or country's favorite pastimes? Are consumers in general more conservative or liberal?

Maybe you think the competitive business environment is important to your decision. Ask yourself: Would it help us to know more about our competitors? Do we need to know how they communicate with their customers? More about their pricing, product features, distribution, and marketing effort? Which new products are on the market and which ones have been well received and why? How do our consumers view the competition? Who dominates the market? Do we need to know the market share of every competitor? Or how mergers and acquisitions affect the competitive environment?

Perhaps information regarding the technological environment will have a strong effect on your business decisions. Ask yourself: Would it help us to know more about the state of technology? Or how consumers are reacting to changes in technology? Do we need to know more about the amount of money the competition is spending on research and development? Or which consumer market segments are the most technology savvy? Do we need to know what technological developments are on the horizon?

MANY MARKETING RESEARCH STUDIES ARE UNDERTAKEN BEFORE ANYONE DETERMINES PRECISELY WHAT IT IS THEY WANT TO LEARN!

It's also essential you carefully examine the individual components of your marketing mix—product, price, place, and promotion. That way, you will be able to determine what information you need to help you to better satisfy the needs of your target market.

Let's start with product. Ask yourself: What is it we need to know about packaging? Do we need to gather feedback regarding individual product features? Do we know what additional features consumers would like? Which feature is most popular or useful? Which features are considered impractical or not useful? Do we know if customers are satisfied with our product? How is the product actually used? Do we need to gather information about service efficiency? What do we know about consumers' understanding of product warranties or instructions? Do consumers need accessories for our products?

Next, look at determining how price is satisfying your target by asking: Do we need to examine price elasticity? Would it help to analyze competitors' pricing? Do we need to gather information to determine how discounts would affect purchases or how pricing affects our product positioning in the target market's minds? How might our costs change over time?

Place is another marketing mix component your questions can explore: Do we know if customers are satisfied with where we are located? Our hours or days of operation? Our ambiance? The setting? The location's safety? Do we know the best distribution channel (retail, wholesale, or mail order) to sell our new products? Where and how our competitors' products are sold?

It's wise to look for information that can tell you how to make your promotional efforts better fit the target. Ask yourself: How are our customers making decisions? How is our marketing program perceived? Is our advertising generating sales? What do we know about awareness or trial of a new product? Which media are most appropriate for our marketing message? Which magazines do our target customers read? Which TV shows do they watch? Which radio stations do they listen to, and for how many hours a day? How are our competitors' marketing programs perceived? What's the makeup of our competitors' marketing programs? Do we know if our sales quotas are appropriate?

If you need to gather a great deal of information to better satisfy the target market, you'll need to design multiple research projects. First, prioritize and gather the information you believe to be most time-sensitive and critical, then attack the question from different angles. Say, for example, absolutely no one responds to your recent magazine ad campaign. So long as you're confident that your product is of high quality and marketable, you probably need to first test the ad copy with a focus group to determine its clarity and effectiveness. A price sensitivity study might also be in order. Combined, multiple studies can give you a fuller picture.

Before You Waste a Lot of Time,

Find Out If the Information You Need

Already Exists

Whether you need information about elements of your marketing mix or the external environment, start by consulting your own network of contacts to find out what they know. Though this informal network research is not scientific, it will keep you from wasting time and money reinventing the wheel. It will also help you hone your research questions and find relevant secondary data (statistics and information gathered previously for another reason) before launching research studies.

When gathering information to help determine a marketing decision, Charlie Trotter believes the best place to start is with your employees. Besides assembling, stocking, packaging, selling, and repairing your products, they provide service and are in the closest and steadiest contact with your customers. They also have lots of opinions they're probably dying to share.

When you need information to make pricing decisions, ask employees: What customer comments have you heard regarding our prices? Have you observed customers mulling over prices? What is the most common reaction? What customer comments have you heard regarding our competitors' pricing? How do you believe prices affect demand? Based on what you've heard, do customers believe our prices are consistent with our product and service positioning?

If it's product information you need, you'll want to ask employees: What customer comments have your heard or reactions have you observed regarding our product's design and packaging? Its features? Warranties? Instructions for use or assembly? Uses? Accessories? What do customers say about competitors' product features, warranties, uses, and accessories?

To learn more about promotion and place, ask staff members: What customer comments have you heard regarding the quality, frequency, and impact of our advertising? Direct mail? Sales efforts? What insight can you offer regarding advertising, direct mail, and our sales program? What customer comments have you heard regarding the competition's marketing efforts? What do customers say about our store location, distribution, delivery, or mail-order service?

Vendors can be very valuable sources of information, too. To gather data on any or all components of your marketing mix, ask vendors how your offering compares with the competition's and what similar and different practices they have observed in the marketplace. To get an idea of how your sales compare with the competition's on a daily, monthly, or seasonal basis, informally ask your parcel carrier, shipper, or product vendors, for example. Vendors also can offer useful observations regarding the local economy and competitive environment.

Before you start gathering data, call a few industry observers and present your potential marketing opportunity or marketing mix problem. For example, an aspiring retailer could call a local newspaper or magazine business writer to learn the state and health of the market, the competition's strengths and weaknesses, the best competitors and products on the market and the reasons why they're best, how the competition markets itself, and the most desirable locations or distribution methods. Though some journalists might be reluctant to provide information on specific companies, most will be happy to speak about industry trends.

Secondary Sources

After you've learned all you can from your personal network of contacts, it's time to turn to data sources. Many highly informative secondary data sources are available to entrepreneurs on the Internet and at libraries and bookstores. Check out *A Guide to Consumer Markets* (The Conference Board), which annually publishes data on consumer behavior and statistics on population, income, employment, and prices. Another good source is the *Sales and Marketing Management Survey of Buying Power* (Sales and Marketing Management), which annually reports consumer buying power by county and city. *Standard & Poor's Industry Surveys* (Standard & Poor's Corp.) is an excellent entree into industry-specific information, including trend analysis and prognostications. As there are countless secondary data sources, the guidebook *Business Information: How to Find It, How to Use It* (Oryx Press) will prove a lifesaver.

Most trade magazines commission or at least report research findings related to their industries. To begin, call the editors at industry magazines and ask if they have published the data you need or know where to find it. To find their phone numbers and addresses, the Bacon's Directories (available on CD-ROM and in reference books at local libraries) list every U.S. media outlet, including magazines, newspapers, and TV and radio stations, according to the subject matter on which they report or the market or geographic region they serve. In the magazine directory, food professionals will find sections on the restaurant industry, food and wine, grocery, confections, and snacks, for example.

Governmental agencies, such as the Small Business Administration and the U.S. Bureau of the Census, report survey findings regularly. The *Census of Retail Trade, Census of Service Industries, Census of Manufacturers,* and *Census of Population* offer valuable statistics. Retailers could turn to the *Census of Retail Trade,* which is taken every five years, to gather information regarding retail sales, employment statistics, and the number of stores in a particular county or city. The *Census of Population,* taken every ten years, reports the population according to geographic regions and includes demographics such as income, gender, family size, education, and race.

An important rule of thumb when researching: whenever you discover research findings or statistical data reported in a newspaper, magazine, or industry journal, try to obtain the information from the original source. Errors can result from transcribing data. Keep in mind that few conclusions are "objective": raw statistics can be interpreted and manipulated in an endless variety of ways. Furthermore, secondary sources often don't describe the methodology used to gather the information or the reason the study was undertaken in the first place—and these factors can be all-important with regard to the quality of the data. A research study on alcohol consumption administered by a brewing company, for example, will likely produce quite different results from an American Medical Association report on the same subject. A press kit sent out by a fledgling software company will likely present that company's financial success in a very different light than a financial investment firm's independent assessment report.

BESIDES ASSEMBLING, STOCKING, PACKAGING, SELLING, AND REPAIRING YOUR PRODUCTS, [YOUR EMPLOYEES] PROVIDE SERVICE AND ARE IN THE CLOSEST AND STEADIEST CONTACT WITH YOUR CUSTOMERS. THEY ALSO HAVE LOTS OF OPINIONS THEY'RE PROBABLY DYING TO SHARE.

No matter what source you use, scrutinize the data with a fine-tooth comb. Are conclusions consistent with the data? Do the sources explain the collection and sampling methodology? Have they effectively qualified respondents? Is the sample representative of the target population? How was the data collected? Should they have used a different method to collect the data? Is it possible the source has an ax to grind? Is the information presented clearly? It's up to you to make marketing mix decisions based on your assessment of the quality of the study. There's no question about it—you'll save yourself a lot of time and money if you take these steps before commissioning a study.

39 Design and Administer a Research Study

and Use the Info

Secondary data is the fastest and least expensive means of gathering information; just a couple of days spent at the library or over the Internet can net you loads of useful facts and figures. But when you're tackling a major project—say, expansion, introducing a brand new line of products, or taking on a partner firm—secondary data will rarely be enough. When the information you find is skimpy or the data is biased, outdated, or poorly researched, it's time to design and administer a research study to collect *primary* data.

While certain circumstances warrant the hiring of professionals to design a study and conduct research, it's not always necessary or affordable. It is entirely possible to learn how to gather accurate data on your own and train employees to assist you. The plethora of fine books and journals on marketing research include *American Demographics* magazine, the *Harvard Business Review,* the *International Journal of Research in Marketing,* the *Journal of Marketing, Marketing Research: An Applied Orientation* (Prentice Hall, 1993), and *Marketing Research: Methodological Foundations* (Dryden Press, 1991).

Regardless of the information you need, there are several kinds of primary data you can collect. Thankfully, there are only two basic methods to collect it: using a questionnaire or focus group, and observing and recording consumer behavior, actions, and reactions.

Getting Quizzical

Questionnaires make it possible to collect two types of information. The first is *qualitative* data, characterized by in-depth, open-ended responses. Qualitative questions allow respondents to answer in their own words, and at length. The second type of data is *quantitative,* which is obtained by asking questions that aim for straightforward, closed-end responses that can be summarized in numbers—percentages, averages, and statistics. The quantitative method requires respondents to select from yes/no or multiple-choice responses. While each approach yields different results, both can be used in the same study.

You can administer surveys in a variety of ways. Mail questionnaires are the most inexpensive method. The drawbacks are that the response rate is generally low and those who respond are often more biased (they feel very strongly about the subject). Furthermore, because no one can assist respondents in answering, the mailed questions must be especially easy to understand. The alternatives, including personal interviews, telephone interviews, and focus groups, provide the most detailed information and have much stronger response rates; however, they also tend to be more expensive.

Because it's impossible to gather information about the entire population you are interested in, you need to study a sample or a subset of the population. Your aim is to ensure that it adequately represents the population you want to study. The key to success is to randomly survey respondents and qualify them according to specified variables, such as demographics and lifestyle. For example, to determine where his target market dines and why, Charlie Trotter could call every hundredth name in the local phone book and interview only heads of household who are over age forty-five, earn more than $150,000 per year, and spend at least $600 a month on dining away from home.

ONCE YOU'VE GATHERED ALL THIS INFORMATION, BE PREPARED FOR SURPRISING RESULTS—RESULTS THAT MAY CHALLENGE YOUR MOST CAREFUL STRATEGIES AND BEST-LAID PLANS.

The most common way to determine consumer opinions on your product, product features, service, price, promotion, location, and your competitors' products is through quantitative research. To collect numerical data, ask customers to rate marketing mix variables on a scale of 1 (poor) to 5 (excellent) or ask them to agree or disagree with various statements. If you have many questions to ask or you want to allow customers to reply anonymously, use a mail questionnaire.

Charlie Trotter's exhaustively asks guests for their opinions, and as a result the restaurant is better able to tailor its marketing mix to its target. In addition to the verbal feedback received by the floor personnel at the restaurant, *all* diners are given satisfaction surveys asking them to rate the food, service, ambiance, and wine list in terms of quality, price, efficiency, aesthetics, attention to detail, and execution. Diners can complete the simple questionnaire before they leave or return the self-addressed, stamped survey at their convenience.

Customer responses are vital to Charlie Trotter's continuous improvement, and they are greatly appreciated. "Guest satisfaction surveys help us to make decisions, from lighting to the pace of the meal to the number of courses to attitude of service staff to pricing of the wine list," says Trotter.

To continuously improve your marketing techniques, you need to know if consumers have seen your advertisements; remember what they've read; know where your store is located; are familiar with your company's products, their distinctive features, and how they're used; and understand how to purchase the products. Familiarity is difficult to observe, so to gauge unaided awareness, ask your sample population qualitative questions (a phone or personal interview is best to gather this kind of data). A Charlie Trotter's survey might ask: What kind of food is served at Charlie Trotter's? How much does it cost to eat at Charlie Trotter's? Where is Charlie Trotter's located?

Except for the daytime talk show set, few of us enjoy blabbing about private matters to perfect strangers. If you want to get real answers when asking respondents sensitive questions about their economic security and status, lifestyle, health, needs, and other personal information, use a mail questionnaire containing mostly quantitative questions. Don't ask them to provide open answers in their own words. Answering these honestly makes most people uncomfortable and closemouthed.

Sharpening Your Eyesight

Sometimes you'll need information regarding purchase and use behavior in order to make marketing mix decisions. You might want to know where a product is most often purchased, where it is used, by whom, under what circumstances, how often, for what purpose, and so on. To study past behavior, you'll have to use a questionnaire. Much of current activity, though, can be observed. Charlie Trotter, for example, could observe customers dining at his restaurant, then compare the setup to one of his competitor's to determine if he should adjust his marketing mix or reconsider his target market. He could observe what they order, how they pay, how much they eat, how much they talk, what features they like, the manner in which they eat, and any number of other behaviors.

Retail businesses especially can benefit from customer observation. Whether observing customers at the point of purchase or watching them make decisions in the aisles, you can determine if lighting is sufficient, if signage and point-of-purchase coupons are effective, if displays and shelving units are easily reached, and if products are effectively cross-promoted, among other things.

Evaluating the Results

Once you've gathered all this information, be prepared for surprising results—results that may challenge your most careful strategies and best-laid plans. Whatever you do, don't conclude that "customers don't really know what they're talking about." Instead, analyze it carefully, share it with your staff, make changes and improvements, and innovate. At Charlie Trotter's, the managers, sommeliers, several cooks, the sous chefs, assistant sous chefs, pastry chef, and office staff study the data. The front line is best equipped to find solutions to customer concerns, so it's important they see what customers think about products, price, promotion, and place. As with your business, raw data provides the fodder for innovation and improvement.

When It Comes to Publicity,

Only a Sharpshooter Will Do

Today, there are few food professionals, food and wine lovers, and business travelers in the United States who do not know about Charlie Trotter and his accomplishments both in the kitchen and on the bottom line. The chef and his restaurant have been featured in broadcast venues ranging from "Good Morning America" and "Oprah" to print media such as the *New York Times, Vogue, USA Today, Esquire,* the *Times* of London, *People, Forbes, Gourmet, Wine Spectator,* and *Chicago* magazine, to name but a fraction of the coverage.

So which came first—the chicken or the egg? Inarguably, Charlie Trotter's could not have been profiled so regularly and exuberantly by so many influential media outlets if the restaurant were not one of the best in the United States. On the other hand, Trotter's has not been heralded simply because it strives for excellence. Trotter has publicized his restaurant methodically, persistently, and, most important, *passionately,* for over eleven years.

As much as some professional publicists might hate to admit it, Charlie Trotter's proves it's possible for an entrepreneur to successfully perform a company's media relations in-house. While many restaurants and small firms hire public relations companies, Trotter actually performs most publicist duties himself. In his view, outside public relations agencies could never express his vision and story ideas with the same passion and enthusiasm.

The trumpeter's task for your company may very likely be no small duty, yet it's difficult to argue that anyone knows your business as well as you do. But be forewarned: it will take a great deal of your time and patience. Furthermore, you'll need to hire at least one or two individuals to help you coordinate a marketing program.

Charlie Trotter knows as well as anyone that the best media relations programs take a precisely targeted approach. That means it's time to take out your media P.R. rifle and load it with shells, not grapeshot. Here's what you need to do:

- **Select media with readers, viewers, and listeners who most closely match your target market.**

- **Don't overlook industry trade publications and small, local media.**

- **Read, watch, and listen to the selected media constantly.**

- **Create databases and classify journalists according to subjects they cover.**

- **Develop pitches targeted to specific magazines and decision makers.**

- **Share your story ideas and ask what editors are working on.**

- **Follow through on your promises.**

- **Maintain constant contact with editors and producers.**

The ultimate goal of publicity is to make a positive impression on your target audience as often as possible. Therefore, the first step in your media relations program is to pinpoint the media that best reach your target market. The Bacon's Directories are essential tools in any media relations program. The *Bacon's Newspaper Directory* is organized according to daily and weekly publications, then according to state and city. The *TV and Radio Directory* is organized by national syndication and local outlets, and *Bacon's Magazines Directory* is organized according to subject, such as food and wine, fashion, technology, business, general interest, and news. Every entry in all three directories summarizes the subject matter each media outlet covers and the demographics and psychographics of the readers, viewers, and listeners they serve. You need to choose media that best fit your target market's location, lifestyles, and demographics.

Whatever you do, don't forget about the little guys—trade publications, local newspapers, and local TV stations. The fact is that industry and local recognition can later help you to gain interest from major consumer media, because newspaper and consumer magazine editors and TV producers read industry publications and local papers and watch TV just like everyone else. Even if they don't see the piece or read it when it's published, you will be able to send them a story clipping or a videocassette.

After you select the media that can best reach your target, you need to familiarize yourself with their editorial and program content, their tone and style, and the work of regular columnists. Subscribe to and read as many of these publications as you can; watch TV news programs whenever you get an opportunity. You can also phone selected companies and request their media kits to learn their editorial missions and plans. Whatever you do, look for thematic patterns and take careful notes as to the distinctions between different outlets. For instance, some food magazines, such as *Fine Cooking,* focus on teaching culinary techniques, while others, such as *Gourmet,* are more interested in fine dining.

TROTTER HAS PUBLICIZED HIS RESTAURANT METHODI-CALLY, PERSISTENTLY, AND, MOST IMPORTANT, **PASSION-ATELY,** FOR OVER ELEVEN YEARS.

Look through back issues of your target magazines, and speak with programming managers from the television and radio stations you're interested in. You must find out which stories your target media have already published, so that you don't pitch the same ideas (doing so is not only a waste of time, but also leaves the impression you're a sloppy researcher).

So that you can develop a mailing or call list quickly and easily, create databases and group entries according to subject matter and geographic location. For each media contact, enter a personal name, title, company name, address, phone and fax numbers, e-mail address, and brief descriptions of the subjects covered. Trotter has discovered it's vital to frequently update databases with new contacts and to correct names and addresses when they change. Here's an example of an entry:

> William Rice, Food and Wine Columnist, *Chicago Tribune,* 435 N. Michigan Ave., Chicago, IL 60611; phone, fax, and e-mail
>
> Notes: writes about food and wine, reviews cookbooks and wines, reports on restaurant and food industry trends, occasionally profiles chefs in Sunday *Tribune Magazine* and contributes to *GQ, Bon Appétit,* and *Food & Wine* (Chicago, Food & Wine Press)

Once you've figured out who's who in the world of media and you've created your database, it's time to start developing ideas and then pitching stories. One approach is to identify publications or electronic media you believe can deliver your target audience and develop story ideas that fit their format. Another approach is to develop your own story ideas and figure out which media and journalists will be most interested in each. Either way, you need to provide ideas that are fresh, exciting, alluring, and specific. Most important, the information you provide editors needs to be of interest to them and their readers, listeners, or viewers.

Trotter used both approaches to publicize his second book, *Charlie Trotter's Vegetables. Food & Wine, Bon Appétit, Saveur, Wine Spectator,* and *Gourmet* magazines best reach Charlie Trotter's target market of affluent food and wine lovers, so he pitched their editors on cooking and dining trend stories. He also believed vegetable cooking would appeal to health- and fitness-conscious consumers and women in particular. In order to reach these audiences, he pitched his idea to food editors at *Vogue, Elle, Allure, Cosmopolitan, Mirabella,* and *W* magazines.

"These magazines write about romantic and hot subjects. And vegetable cooking is perfect for their readers, who want to eat healthfully and look sexy," explains Trotter. The road to quality coverage was a rocky one. "Nine out of ten fashion magazine food editors were not interested, but one was: Jeffrey Steingarten at *Vogue.* We've had contact with Jeffrey over the years; he's dined here and I know him. He called to say, 'I don't generally write about restaurants, but that is a great subject. I want to do it.'"

Publicity-savvy entrepreneurs like Trotter know personal calls are the most effective way to talk to media decision-makers and learn what stories are in the works. After you confirm that the editor or producer has the time to listen, offer your story idea. It's especially helpful to make references to past stories they have published or broadcast; doing so indicates you know what they cover and can suggest an idea that will fit both their style and editorial mission.

Breaking in is a tough job, and it takes tenacity. More than likely, you won't succeed on the first try. No matter what, bite your tongue and listen to their explanation as to why the idea doesn't fit. As you build a rapport with members of the media, you will be able to ask them what kinds of stories they're working on to determine how you might provide useful information.

Above all, do what you say you're going to do. When you promise to submit a written proposal or background materials to an editor, comply. When you promise to call them or be available for an interview on a specific day, don't forget. Because of schedules in the media world, editors and producers don't have time for unreliable publicists and sources. Disappoint them once, and you might burn a bridge.

Though it's wise not to call busy journalists more than once a month, it's essential you keep in contact with key media players on a regular basis. Over time, they'll appreciate your determination and zeal. In addition, constant contact with media will keep you and your company present in the minds of reporters and editors in a very competitive business environment. When they need to find a source for a story or a subject to profile, they'll be more likely to call you. Be gracious, meticulously careful with your comments, and, above all, open-minded. If you start to be considered an exciting and knowledgeable resource, you're in the big leagues. You're success as a publicist will skyrocket.

41 Conventional Press Releases

Aren't Worth the Postage

Press releases are a great way to notify media VIPs about upcoming events, relocation, simple new product introductions, awards received, sales promotions, and the like. These timely, single-page statements tell the who, what, when, why, and where of your upcoming event or product. Catchy, fact-rich, and concise, the best press releases often show up as small blurbs in local newspaper and magazine articles.

However, press releases are an extremely *ineffective* way to pitch specific feature stories. Your number-one job as a publicist is to intimately understand which media best reach your target audience and then to provide story ideas that appeal to their readership, listeners, or viewers. Because press releases are mailed to a range of media contacts at once, the slant is general, rather than specific. In other words, it's not aimed at any particular readership—an essential component if you're planning to land a story. On top of that, editors and producers are so constantly inundated with other press releases that it will be next to impossible to rise above the clutter churned out by competitors.

To get beyond these obstacles and convey story ideas to editors and producers, Charlie Trotter's writes personal letters and customizes its own press kits. The restaurant makes a sizable investment in beautifully crafted and packaged ideas, but the return is also great. The fact is, publicity is one of the most affordable and cost-effective ways to communicate information to your target audience.

Luckily, there's a method to the madness—at least at Trotter's. The media team follows ten basic steps to create and distribute informative, attractive press kits:

- **Write a company positioning statement.**
- **Write biographies of key players.**
- **Prepare lists of products and services.**
- **Gather supporting materials, such as testimonials and citations.**
- **Prepare a fact sheet.**
- **Order reprints of newspaper and magazine clippings or prepare color photocopies.**
- **Commission four-color photography of products, principals, and place.**
- **Attach personal cover letters and mail the press kits.**
- **Target mailings.**
- **Follow up.**

When dealing with the media, first impressions are crucial. Because editors and TV and radio producers receive hundreds of pieces of mail per week, it's vital that every component of your presentation be creative, compelling, well-conceived, and professionally executed, reflecting your vision and values.

Remember, when editors and producers receive your press kits, the first thing they'll see is the envelope and presentation cover. Unless you have a talented and experienced graphic artist and designer on staff, pay an outside firm or individual to create an eye-catching, unconventional package. First, interview candidates for the graphics project. After selecting a talented artist who meets your standards, meet with her personally to discuss the contents, your vision, and your company's culture and personality. Let her propose a choice of colors, styles, designs, and presentation vehicles. After you agree on a look that suits your company, print at least several hundred folders, jackets, or covers with your company logo and envelopes, plus several hundred pieces of letterhead.

While the designer is working on the presentation vehicle, you or one of your employees should write a company positioning statement. This document—no more than five double-spaced pages—must communicate the attributes that set you apart from the competition, product and place highlights, and recent developments, plus accomplishments and accolades. It also should include company vitals (name, address, hours of operation, contact names, fax number, and e-mail and Web site addresses) and mention how long you've been in business. Inserting favorable quotes from industry experts or observers about your company will help support your statements.

Editors and producers also need to know something about you and other key players in your organization in order to make decisions. To make their jobs easier, prepare separate, one-page biographies for insertion in the press kit. Bios should include the person's influences, background, qualifications, relevant experience and training, education, and awards and accomplishments. It's also helpful to include human-interest information about the person's family, hobbies, interests, and cause-related efforts.

Journalists in particular appreciate lists or catalogs of the products and services your company provides. Charlie Trotter's press kits include a recent menu, a wine list, a list of the restaurant's consulting assignments, and a brief description of retail products. For fairly complex products, you should provide detailed information, such as features, benefits, and warranty information, rather than simple lists. You need to have all the documents neatly typeset and printed in a catalog or on letterhead for inclusion in press kits.

You should also gather any other supporting materials the media might find useful. Whether it's product labels, a book jacket, a safety report, a citation from an industry association, testimonials from customers, an annual report, or a recommendation from the King of Spain, obtain copies of all supporting materials to include in your kits. Be sure these materials are of the same quality as all the other components in your presentation package.

Good press kits always include a fact sheet, too. Basically, it's a thumbnail sketch of the positioning statement, which an editor or producer can read quickly. This one-page, single-spaced document should also list company vitals, as in the positioning statement, but in the shortest, most accessible form.

The most persuasive and objective documents you'll include in the press kit are press clippings. These should be collected well in advance: every time your business is mentioned or profiled in an important newspaper or magazine, order 500 reprints from the publisher. If you clip stories yourself, you need to have them color-photocopied. Remember, a clip must include the publication masthead, date of publication, and, ideally, an enlargement of the section of the article in which you are profiled. After you accumulate several such clips, choose the ones that are most relevant and influential. For example, a *New York Times* cover story will have a greater impact than a local suburban newspaper clipping.

When compiling your press kits, remember that pictures do speak louder than words. Particularly if your building, interior, or products have eye-catching design elements, commissioning four-color photography for your press kits is an immeasurably smart investment. As an added bonus, provide pictures of yourself and key players—journalists often need to profile talented or interesting individuals. To promote his books, Charlie Trotter includes eight-by-ten-inch, four-color prints of his culinary creations to illustrate their originality, quality, and stunning beauty. Though magazines and newspapers often end up assigning their own staff photographers to shoot specific pictures for an article, the photographs you send will attract them in the first place.

To top off your press package, write personalized one-page cover letters, print them on company letterhead, and clip them to the front cover of each kit. This is your main opportunity to present story ideas to specific editors and producers and persuade them to pursue your idea. As with a feature story, your lead is vital. You need to propose your compelling, targeted story idea in the first paragraph and sell it. Whatever you do, don't be shy or vague. Refer to materials you've included in the kit. Provide supporting information. End the letter by mentioning that you'll follow up in two weeks and offer a telephone number where you can be reached in the meantime. Don't forget to keep a copy of the letter on your computer for future reference.

Once presentation packages are designed and printed, you're ready to mail the press kits. That

BECAUSE EDITORS AND TV AND RADIO PRODUCERS RECEIVE HUNDREDS OF PIECES OF MAIL PER WEEK, IT'S VITAL THAT EVERY COMPONENT OF YOUR PRESENTATION BE CREATIVE, COMPELLING, WELL-CONCEIVED, AND PROFESSIONALLY EXECUTED, REFLECTING YOUR VISION AND VALUES.

means it's time to target mailings. You want to tailor the contents of your press kits to each media audience: news, fashion, sports, lifestyle, general interest, trade, and specialty broadcasters and publications should each receive *customized* press kits. Include information that will be of most interest to the editor or producer and to the audience. Weed out unnecessary fluff—it'll only keep them from taking the bait. In press kits mailed to wine writers, for example, Charlie Trotter's wouldn't include information on its consulting services. Trotter knows that wine scribes couldn't care less about his opinions on how to set up a 3,000-square-foot kitchen or which fish companies he uses. Remember what your target wants and feed them all the information you can on that subject.

The last but most important step is to follow up by phone. Whenever possible, politely but firmly request to speak with the editor or producer whom you've targeted—not an intern or assistant. If they're not available at the moment, try back later. Once you do get the head honcho on the line, make sure you're poised, confident, and succinct. "Did you receive my company press kit?" is *not* a strong opening line. Assume that the producer or editor has received your kit; ask if she has a moment to talk, and get to the point. Reiterate your pitch briefly, offer to provide other materials if necessary, and ask if she'd like to arrange an interview. Even if she can't use your idea, she'll have you on file as a resource for future reference. And you never know when big news will break, giving the person you courted good reason to call you up.

Like every other aspect of your business, your press kit should not be a static entity. Be willing to change, update, and improve it frequently to keep it fresh and current. Though it takes plenty of time and energy to assemble professional press kits and make dozens of phone calls, they're far more effective than press releases. Once your company is featured in several papers and magazines, you'll realize the true value of your effort.

React Quickly When Crises Arise

to Avoid Bad Publicity

Let's imagine you're the proud owner of an admirably successful fresh juice enterprise, intent upon providing an increasingly health-conscious public with pure, direct-from-the-fruit beverages. You started out twenty years ago, small and idealistic. Elixirs of mango and papaya, pineapple, and fresh-squeezed oranges seduced an original loyal following. Your chlorophyll- and vitamin-rich wheat grass, beet, and carrot concoctions and wacky, wild, neo-primitive designer labels gained you an even larger customer base. Your business's future couldn't look sweeter.

Then your worst nightmare becomes a reality: reports surface that a batch of your product—simple unpasteurized apple juice—is contaminated with *E. coli* bacteria, causing the death of a small child and a number of other customers to fall seriously ill. What you don't know is how many stores locally or nationally might be stocking the tainted juice. The bottom line: you're going to have to act deftly and decisively if there's any hope of saving your business. You've got a major public health crisis on your hands.

This actually happened to the California-based juice company Odwalla in 1996. Thanks to its immediate, effective, and concerned public relations campaign, the company was able to overcome the tragedy and maintain its loyal customer following.

While perilous public safety crises like the aforementioned are somewhat rare, you need to be prepared for the countless and not uncommon public relations challenges that your small business may face—challenges few entrepreneurs consider in advance. What sort of challenges? Imagine if you or someone in your company were to be accused—rightly or wrongly—of sexual harassment, tax evasion, embezzlement, hiring illegal aliens, or unfair business practices. The list of what companies have faced goes on, from the merely irritating to the bizarre: indeed, Procter & Gamble was even wrongly accused of Satan worship several years ago. Whether you're faced with public health crises or charges of wrongdoing, there are several steps you need to take:

- **React quickly before bad publicity is generated.**
- **Assemble a team of industry experts and peers to help you formulate a plan.**
- **Assign one company spokesperson to handle the media and public relations.**
- **Notify the media quickly.**
- **When you don't know certain information, don't guess.**
- **Recommend outside industry experts and sources for media.**
- **Draft a written response and set up a toll-free hot line to answer questions.**
- **Take steps to resolve the problem or crisis.**
- **Quash rumors.**

When your business is facing a crisis or emergency of public health or safety, no matter what is going on in your life or work, you need to drop everything and address the problem immediately. The reasons are practical as well as ethical. First, when you wait too long to react, someone may be injured. Second, the public may conclude you're guilty or negligent. And finally, the media may cry "cover-up" and your company's reputation can be quickly destroyed. React quickly because it's the right thing to do *and* because your story is more likely to be considered credible than if you delay.

It's wise to have an emergency plan in place before crises arise, but even with an advance plan, it's a good idea to assemble a team of industry experts to provide you with information when you are faced with a crisis. With respect to public safety or health risks, you will need to know the specific dangers, symptoms of illness, the worst-case scenarios, and the steps to be taken in an emergency. You might need to consult public health officials, the Centers for Disease Control and Prevention, physicians, or the Red Cross. For less serious upsets—for example, legal ones—gather industry peers, public relations experts, and attorneys to discuss the issues and ask their advice. They may well have encountered similar situations and have valuable insights to share.

Whatever you do, make sure only one person in your company (probably you) is charged with assembling all the relevant information and communicating with the public and the media. The worst thing that could happen in a crisis or emergency is to have conflicting stories emanating from your company. The media will be all over inconsistencies like flies on dung. You need to instruct all your staff and anyone affiliated with your company to refer all customers, consumer advocacy or public interest groups, law-enforcement officers, and media to the spokesperson.

If you confirm there are bona fide public health and safety issues or other crises, you need to notify the media immediately. First of all, you should send media alerts by fax or call the news desks of major TV network affiliates, radio stations, and newspapers to call a press conference in order to explain to them what you have discovered. In some cases, you might even notify the Emergency Broadcast System. The point person candidly should tell reporters everything he or she knows about the case and provide records or leads if possible. Whatever you do, don't hold anything back. Tell them everything you know about casualties, damages, causes, dangers, risks, and so on. Most important, warn the public not to consume or use your product until the situation is resolved.

No matter what, you or your company spokesperson should

never speculate about any aspect of the crisis and should only share confirmed or corroborated information with the media. When a reporter asks a question and you honestly don't know the answer, say: "We don't have that information at this time." Simply make it clear the company and appropriate public officials are investigating the situation and steps are being taken to ensure public health and safety, such as removing the product from store shelves nationally.

Particularly in cases of public health and safety, it's smart to refer the media to outside industry experts and sources with whom you are in contact, such as engineers, scientists, physicians, or health department officials. Let's face it: they're better equipped to answer questions. You also should provide the names of regular customers, business associates, journalists, or industry observers, who can vouch for your integrity and attention to detail.

After you share your story with the media, you can bet you're going to get plenty of phone calls from other media and customers. To answer questions, you might draft a letter to explain the situation and the steps you are taking to resolve the problem. So that callers don't have to leave messages on voicemail, which will give them a negative impression of your response to the crisis, set up a toll-free hot line with operators who will take messages, direct calls, or offer to send information by mail.

In order to do the right thing and convince the public and

> . . . BE PREPARED FOR THE COUNTLESS AND NOT UNCOMMON PUBLIC RELATIONS CHALLENGES THAT YOUR SMALL BUSINESS MAY FACE— CHALLENGES FEW ENTREPRENEURS CONSIDER IN ADVANCE.

media you are truly concerned, you need to take definite steps to resolve problems or crises. With respect to legal matters, you might hire an investigator to determine if individuals in your company are guilty of wrongdoing or offer to provide company records for outside inspection. When it comes to ensuring public safety and health, you might fix product defects, exchange products, or provide full product refunds. You might even offer free medical exams to customers who fear they have consumed or used a product that could cause injury or illness. The fresh juice manufacturer would be advised to pull all the products off store shelves and recall all juice purchased over the past two months, for example.

In the middle of a crisis or other serious situation, you certainly don't want rumors to circulate. Where and how they start might never be discovered, but one thing's for sure: you need to quash rumors immediately. The best way to handle unsubstantiated reports is to invite industry experts, authorities, and the media to investigate. Say, for example, your restaurant is accused of serving hamburgers contaminated with an unmentionable foreign substance. Provided you know the claims are untrue, the restaurant spokesperson should invite the local health department and the media to inspect the facilities, products, preparation methods, and sanitation procedures.

A few years ago, Charlie Trotter learned that Chicago's Health Department was considering shutting down his "chef's table"—the coveted behind-the-scenes seating where special guests view Trotter's team preparing culinary masterpieces as they eat. The city argued that customers with a contagious disease seated at the chef's table could spread the disease through the food served to other customers.

Trotter reacted decisively and quickly. First he called a meeting that day with his staff to explain the situation and to inform them he would be the sole spokesperson. Next, he called local and national TV news producers; business and news desks at the *Chicago Tribune,*

Chicago Sun-Times, and other local newspapers; plus several news and trade magazine editors. The chef-owner told the press everything he knew about the situation and the precautions he takes to ensure diner safety and health. At the same time he respectfully addressed the city's concerns. Trotter smartly invited the media to examine his operation firsthand. And they did.

Reporters were in and out of his kitchen for the next week, scrutinizing, asking him questions, taking notes, filming. Not only did he provide a full behind-the-scenes look, he also provided the names of peers, customers, and industry experts, who could provide their opinions and expertise. In less than a week, the *Chicago Tribune* and *Sun-Times,* CNN-TV, and every local TV news program had reported on the case and had portrayed Trotter as a quality-driven sanitation standard-bearer. Rather than hurt business, supportive letters and calls poured into the restaurant for weeks and reservations were better than ever.

Ultimately, the Health Department backed off when it felt the heat from the public, media, and local politicians, who feared Trotter might pack up his world-class restaurant and move to another city. Rather than hide, Trotter had aggressively welcomed the scrutiny and provided the information media and consumers needed. Lesson learned. Not only does a proactive approach help you to avoid bad publicity, but often your efforts will help to improve your company image, too.

Develop a Targeted Marketing
Database of Customers

Ever wonder why most product warranty cards ask you to answer a long list of seemingly irrelevant questions? It's because manufacturers often plan to sell the data to another marketer or use the information to market directly to you in the future. In an excellent business, a well-managed data system is an essential component of a successful direct marketing strategy. No matter how beautiful your direct-mail pieces or how exciting your product videos are, direct marketing won't be effective if it doesn't reach the right consumers.

For several years, on a monthly basis, Charlie Trotter's hosted guest chef engagements, seasonal food festivals, wine dinners, and anniversary celebrations. Emeril Lagasse, Jean-Louis Palladin, David Bouley, Gray Kunz, and others—many of the best chefs in the United States—were involved in these events. Other evenings the star was a food ingredient itself, featured in multicourse dinners. Occasionally, winemakers and their products were also under the spotlight. The $100- to $150-per-person events usually were held on Tuesdays or Wednesdays, typically slow nights in restaurants. What's amazing is that almost every event sold out.

Interestingly, the restaurant's primary objective in hosting these events was not to fill the restaurant on slow nights. Rather, the high-profile performances were created to help to position Charlie Trotter's as one of the finest restaurants in the country. To accomplish this objective, it was essential that the events were not only trend-setting, but also well attended. Without a well-filled dining room, the dinners never would have created a buzz in the media or among food and wine lovers.

Naturally, Trotter publicized the events to local and national media, since editorial coverage positions a product or service and helps to generate sales. But Trotter knows publicity is not the only way to drive business. For starters, he knew that only some media outlets would cover each story. Additionally, no matter how well particular media reach the target market, there is always "waste coverage." In other words, publications, TV programs, or radio shows will reach many consumers who are not part of your target market. That's why Trotter also used direct marketing to reach specific customers, potential clients, and potentially valuable media contacts to make the most of these gala events.

With a good database, direct marketing is one of the most effective ways to communicate with a target audience to generate a desired response, whether that's a store visit or a sale. To develop a useful database, you will need to gather a variety of information from your customers, including their names, addresses, phone numbers, demographics, lifestyle data, and needs. Unlike typical research studies, the goal is to collect basic information from as many customers as possible.

Besides warranty cards, you can use applications for credit cards, frequent customer programs, and customer comment cards to learn the age, income, sex, marital status, family size, hobbies, activities, interests, and needs of your customers. Tracking these vitals can save resources. As an example, for years, the author of this book received weekly direct-mail pieces from a company promoting quality roofing services and offering free carpet cleaning—even though he lived in an apartment complex with wood floors. Clearly, these marketers didn't have a database management plan like Charlie Trotter's.

You also need to track customer purchases to better market to your target. Keep tabs on what customers purchase; the time of day, week, or year; the amount they purchase; how often they purchase specific items; if they purchase complementary items; if they use coupons; if they shop during special promotions; what method they use to pay; and, if possible, why they purchased specific items.

The next step is to capture and combine all the customer background information and purchase history and organize entries in your database using keywords. This is one of the best reasons to encourage customers to apply for store credit cards or "preferred customer" cards. That way, purchase information and customer data is captured automatically at the checkout counter. Even if you have to input all the information manually, it's well worth the investment. You should use keywords such as "affluent," "suburban," "parent," "teenager," "single," "style trendsetter," "heavy user," "frequent customer," "deep discount shopper," and so on. Trotter, for example, could categorize his restaurant customers according to the wines they order, the amount of money they spend, the frequency with which they visit the restaurant, and if they dine for special or business occasions.

To market to potential customers, it's a great idea to purchase lists from magazines that best reach your target market. *Food & Wine* magazine and other food publications sell their circulation lists for about $90 per thousand names on average. They also capture informa-

PUBLICATIONS, TV PROGRAMS, OR RADIO SHOWS WILL REACH MANY CONSUMERS WHO ARE NOT PART OF YOUR TARGET MARKET. THAT'S WHY TROTTER ALSO USE DIRECT MARKETING TO REACH SPECIFIC CUSTOMERS, POTENTIAL CLIENTS, AND POTENTIALLY VALUABLE MEDIA CONTACTS TO MAKE THE MOST OF THESE GALA EVENTS.

tion, such as demographics and purchasing habits, including whether or not the reader purchases food via mail order. Trotter could purchase highly affluent names to market his restaurant and a list of mail-order purchasers to market his books and recently released food products. Call the media who best reach your target market and ask them to refer you to their list broker for details.

You can also purchase lists of customers from a variety of services, including credit-card companies, mortgage lenders, manufacturers, retailers, and telemarketing companies. To find the right lists for your purposes, go to your local library reference section and consult Standard Rates and Data Service's *Direct Mail List Rates and Data*. This multivolume set lists thousands of well-indexed choices from which to choose and the cost per thousand names. More than likely, you'll be able to find what you need.

Chances are, most lists won't perfectly represent your target market. For example, food magazine lists won't tell you which individuals regularly eat in restaurants that cost $135 per person. That's why it's smart to call the individuals on the lists you purchase to further qualify them before you market directly. You might need to gather and confirm lifestyle, purchase behavior, or additional demographic data to determine who best fits your target market characteristics.

Go Ahead, Toot Your Own Horn

Of the five basic methods of promoting your business—direct marketing, public relations, personal sales, sales promotion, and advertising—Charlie Trotter's concentrates its efforts on the first three, with the greatest emphasis and time devoted to publicity. In fact, Trotter does not advertise his restaurant or offer coupons or discounts at all.

While advertising and sales promotion might not be appropriate for a world-class restaurant, these methods are useful and perhaps a necessity for other small businesses and manufactured products. It's unlikely service stations, printing shops, and local convenience stores could benefit much from publicity, unless they are providing extraordinary amenities or services. Most of these businesses rely on ads and sales promotion. And discounts are almost expected from mass merchandise, retail grocery, and department stores, for example. You need to research what methods are most common in your industry, conduct market research to learn how consumers chose your business or type of business in the first place, and determine what method is most cost-effective for you.

There are pros and cons when it comes to advertising and sales promotion. Because you pay for it, advertising offers you control. Unlike publicity, with ads you determine when the information runs, the content, the graphics, the tone, the placement, and the media in which it runs. Unfortunately, ads are pricey, often missed or downright ignored, and usually perceived as biased. Sales promotion, including samples, discounts, and coupons, are a great way to persuade consumers to try your product or service for the first time and to stimulate sales in the short term. The problem is consumers come to expect savings on your product, and discounts probably will cheapen your product's image.

To toot your own horn with any success, you need to present information effectively and attractively. That's why it's critical you obtain the services of a graphic design firm or hire someone with creative talent and excellent computer design skills to work in-house. Creative use of headlines, color, visual effects, illustrations, four-color photography, and the like requires someone with ample experience and training in typesetting and page layout. It's possible to hire a full-time, experienced, highly talented computer artist for about $50,000 per year in major metro areas. Interview artists who have QuarkXPress, Adobe Illustrator, and other design program experience, plus portfolios that demonstrate substantial direct marketing or magazine layout experience. Web-site development experience is very valuable, too. In fact, you ought to assign work to candidates to test their skills on a freelance basis before hiring them.

It seems like everybody has his or her own Web site these days. Nonetheless, that, in and of itself, is one of the worst reasons to launch one. While the Internet is an increasingly popular way to market to consumers internationally, you need to ask yourself some key questions before developing a site: What do I hope to gain from launching a Web site? What are my goals? Is there a better or more effective way to communicate with my target market? Is our company's target market Web savvy? Do we have the personnel to update the site regularly? Do we have the personnel to respond to on-line requests for information? Could I find sponsors or partners who would share the costs?

Should you decide a Web site is the way to go, you'll need to set specific marketing goals for the project. Among other possibilities, your Web site can serve to position your company; inform potential and current customers about product benefits and thereby generate both trial and repeat sales; post a product catalog; boost sales through direct response advertising; provide value-added services, such as background on your company, product applications and evaluations, and research data; or simply give customers a way of checking the availability, price, and features of your products and services via computer from the comfort of their homes.

Charlie Trotter's Web site includes a biography of the chef and the restaurant, awards the restaurant has earned over the years, recipes, photos of culinary offerings and the dining room, information about private parties and events, promotional pieces and ordering information on the chef's six cookbooks, and links to other related restaurant, food, and cookbook sites. Just go to www.charlietrotters.com for a firsthand look at a first-class Web site. And don't forget: though it's possible to accomplish a variety of marketing objectives with one Web site, it's critical that it be easily navigable and straightforward.

Many excellent small businesses use monthly or quarterly newsletters to communicate with their target market. If you have a Shakespeare in residence, have it written in-house. If not, you may need a freelance writer to compose the text. As a marketing tool, you can use a newsletter to position your firm as *the* expert in your field; subtly or directly remind customers to choose your company over your competitors'; educate consumers vis-à-vis industry or company developments (say, scientific breakthroughs, product innovations, or pending legislation); announce prestigious awards that you, employees, and the company receive; and promote upcoming events or product launches.

Video demonstrations will be invaluable if you make or sell luxury goods, technical or high-performance equipment, or provide services that are best understood visually. Car dealerships, health clubs and spas, industrial equipment manufacturers, art galleries, and high-end salons can all market their products via direct-mail video demonstrations. More than likely, you'll hire a production or advertising company to produce a video. Involve yourself in the production, making sure that the video positions your product; effectively demonstrates your product's benefits, features, and distinguishing characteristics; and explains how to purchase it.

In 1997, Trotter converted part of his company's office space into a "studio" kitchen with built-in, easy-to-use video cameras. Besides being able to project cooking demos onto monitors in the classroom, he is able to tape videos to promote his business.

What if your company produces a large variety of items? Design and distribute a four-color catalog and use this direct-mail piece to promote the newest products available, upcoming store appearances (by celebrities, experts, authors, artists, craftspeople, designers), scheduled product demos, special events, store locations and hours, and sales promotions. Your catalog should feature vivid descriptions of features and the key benefits, product photographs or illustrations, accolades and awards, prices, and availability. Also include a mail-order form to sell products via this channel. With the proliferation of lovely mail-order catalogs, you'll have an array of models to scan for ideas. When it comes to artistic presentation, for example, the standard-bearer of Christmas catalogs is Dallas-based Neiman Marcus, whose catalog, with its stunning photography and design, has the production values of a coffeetable book.

TO TOOT YOUR OWN HORN WITH ANY SUCCESS, YOU NEED TO PRESENT INFORMATION EFFECTIVELY AND ATTRACTIVELY.

A very effective way to reach your target market is to develop and distribute unusual, personalized direct-mail pieces, such as personal letters, announcements, and handsome invitations. Charlie

Trotter's uses such direct-mail pieces to announce guest chef appearances, anniversary dinners, renovations, product launches, and book-signing engagements. All are elegantly designed and position the restaurant as a trendsetter.

Specialty advertising, such as trendy shopping bags or postcards embossed with your company logo, is a great way to constantly remind your customers to choose you. In addition, these items promote you to potential customers. Charlie Trotter's gives away stylish cloth baseball caps with the company logo to regular customers, employees, and even journalists. The cap, emblazoned with Trotter's name, has been sighted on joggers running along Chicago's North Shore lakefront and in the Chicago Marathon.

Plan to Sell Your Sole

Why would Charlie Trotter need to partake in personal sales activities? It's not as though gourmet restaurateurs telemarket to consumers, persuading them to dine in their establishments. Yet the fact is, if it weren't for personal sales, Charlie Trotter's probably would be out of business. That's because Chicago's fine-dining community alone cannot support such an upscale, albeit superb, restaurant. In the words of Bill Rice of the *Chicago Tribune,* "Charlie has an expensive restaurant and he can't rely on the neighborhood."

How does he do it, then? For starters, the restaurant sells private parties and catered events to large corporations and smaller businesses, sales which account for a big chunk of annual revenue. Another important group of customers are out-of-towners. Indeed, nearly half the restaurant's customers are from outside the Chicago area. To persuade those with real "pull" over this pool of potential clients, Charlie Trotter's has a number of surefire strategies. For example, the restaurant contacts upscale hotel concierges on a regular basis, inviting them to dine and providing them with convincing press clippings and other publicity materials.

The fact is that personal sales is essential in many small businesses. In some cases it's too expensive or difficult to reach certain narrow segments of buyers with ads and editorial placements. Through advertising alone, for instance, Charlie Trotter's cannot effectively reach personnel who plan corporate parties at major Chicago-area conglomerates or concierges who direct hotel guests to Trotter's establishment.

When you determine personal selling is the best way to market some or all of your products to some or all of your customers, you'll need to determine how many salespeople to hire. To get started, you need to identify how many potential customers are in your market, whether you're considering city, state, country, or the world. This step requires a good deal of research. You'll consult trade magazines, list providers, chambers of commerce, associations, and professional organizations to learn the number of potential customers in a given market. Your research sources will depend on your target market. For example, since Charlie Trotter's primarily services exclusive clientele, the staff wouldn't use the Yellow Pages to prospect for, say, private-party sales. Instead, Trotter's consults the Fortune 500 list, membership lists from the National Restaurant Association and professional associations such as the American Medical Association, and special issues of *Crain's Chicago Business.* From *Crain's,* Trotter's is able to determine the number of Chicago businesses with annual revenues over $20 million and garner essential information about the type of business they conduct, along with CEO names, addresses, and phone and fax numbers.

Obviously, you can't make sales until you reach decision-makers—those who'll actually make a purchase. The best way to determine the amount of time it takes to reach them is to randomly call 50 to 100 potential customers. You might discover it takes 20 hours to reach 100 decision-makers. If you have 5000 potential customers, it will require roughly 1000 hours to reach all the prospects. More than likely, you'll want to reach all these prospects at least once every two or three months. In this model, then, your strategy will require two full-time salespeople.

The next step is to determine the number of decision-makers you need to contact to make a sale and the amount of time required to close a sale. Again, the most accurate method to figure out these numbers is to make about 50 to 100 sales calls. You could also base your estimate on a number of factors, including the type of product you're selling and the level of knowledge about your products or services in the marketplace. A high level of product or service complexity and a low level of product awareness will require a greater number of sales calls. You can determine the market's level of product knowledge with marketing research and, if necessary, increase awareness with advertising, publicity, and direct marketing before launching a personal selling effort.

It's also helpful to estimate the amount of time salespeople will have each week to make sales calls. Consider if they'll have any responsibilities in addition to selling, if the products require a significant amount of customer service, if salespeople will have administrative support, and if they will be expected to teach buyers how to use the products.

Once you've determined the number of salespeople you need, write out job descriptions for each sales position before hiring. Be sure to consider what skills, schooling, experience, and flexibility are necessary for each job. When it's time to interview salespeople, you will want to ask questions mainly to assess their desire. (Recall some of the suggestions from Lesson 6, "Hire for Desire Rather Than Experience.")

After you find employees with the right qualifications and passion, hire them. But before you train them, organize sales territories so they won't be selling the same products to the same customers and so they will have enough customers to call.

The most common sales territories are geographic, while organizing the selling effort according to the type of customers is most appropriate for businesses that sell to many different kinds of buyers. Small businesses that manufacture technical products frequently organize territories according to product type. Depending on how complex your products are, one salesperson might represent a product line or only one product.

Assess your own business and the kind of sales territories that make the most sense. Like every area in business, planning and preparation is key to sales success.

Training Your Sales Staff

Wines are an integral part of the dining experience at Charlie Trotter's, and the ideal pairing of wine with a variety of foodstuffs is one of the restaurant's most creative aspects. Trotter's wine staff serves as guides and, ultimately, salespeople, finding just the right elixir to complement a meal. Their knowledge must be thorough: depending on how it is prepared, ahi tuna might be best served with a champagne or sancerre, or with something fuller, such as a Merlot or a red burgundy. Knowing this, Trotter's sommelier will grill his assistants for hours before they are allowed to recommend and sell wine to diners.

Though the best way to learn how to sell is by selling, you can't turn salespeople loose before they have an intimate understanding of your company's philosophies, products, and policies. Especially if your company manufactures complex products or provides complicated services, employees should work a few months in production, client services, marketing, and customer service to best understand the operation before they sell. For companies whose product features and benefits are limited, a few weeks of training in each department and classroom training is sufficient.

After new hires are able to pass a test to demonstrate thorough product, service, and policy knowledge, it's time to place them in sales positions. Coaching and supervising new salespeople is one of the most effective ways to train, because it allows you or a senior manager to listen to and observe sales presentations and address with trainees needed improvements immediately after sales calls are made. After each sales presentation, you need to evaluate the salesperson's persuasiveness, professionalism, communication of product knowledge, and selling skills, among other things.

Another effective way to train new hires is to stage mock sales presentations. You act as the potential customer and ask new hires to sell your company's products or services to you. Ask difficult questions to determine their knowledge of product benefits and features, drill them on company policies and terms, tell them you can't afford their products, and say you have enough of whatever they're selling and you're not ready to buy for several months. Basically, challenge them to sell.

To teach selling skills, many entrepreneurs enlist the help of experts. Depending on your budget and your sales training ability, you might choose to send your employees to sales seminars locally or nationally, or feature sales training videos in company meetings. The American Marketing Association in Chicago, for example, can provide information on sales seminars and videos, and the larger video-rental chains have sections devoted to professional training and improvement.

Regardless of how you train your employees, there are six steps salespeople need to take in order to make sales and encourage repeat business:

• **Identify potential customers.**

• **Approach the appropriate individuals.**

- Determine if there is a sales possibility.

- Make the sale.

- Close the sale.

- Follow up.

The first step is to identify potential customers, using the same methods suggested earlier in this lesson. Next, after identifying which businesses or individuals are potential customers, it's important to initiate relationships with these people. It's your sales staff's job to identify decision-makers and create some initial interest in your product. To sell food products to a hotel, for example, salespeople might need to contact a purchasing agent, food and beverage manager, and executive chef. Train your salespeople to first consult directories to determine who the buyers are and, as a last resort, ask to speak with the person responsible for making purchasing decisions.

Once salespeople know who calls the shots at each company or residence, they need to figure out if the prospect is worth pursuing: Does the prospective client have a binding contract or relationship with another supplier? Does he truly need your company's product? Will he benefit from it? Is he able to pay for it, and purchase enough volume to make it worth your company's effort? Will he continue to need it? When pursuing potential banquet or private-party clients, Charlie Trotter's salespeople ask how much that company spends per person for meals, how many off-site parties it has per year, and if the company requires particular accommodations as a prerequisite.

When salespeople are convinced prospects qualify, it's time to persuade the prospects to become customers. One of the most effective approaches is to research and analyze prospect businesses, identify needs and opportunities, address these needs with buyers in meetings, and convince them your product or service best satisfies their needs. To convince buyers your product is best suited for their

IN SOME CASES IT'S TOO EX-
PENSIVE OR DIFFICULT TO
REACH CERTAIN NARROW
SEGMENTS OF BUYERS WITH
ADS AND EDITORIAL PLACE-
MENTS. THROUGH ADVERTIS-
ING ALONE, FOR INSTANCE,
CHARLIE TROTTER'S CANNOT
EFFECTIVELY REACH PERSON-
NEL WHO PLAN CORPORATE
PARTIES AT MAJOR CHICAGO-
AREA CONGLOMERATES OR
CONCIERGES WHO DIRECT HO-
TEL GUESTS TO TROTTER'S ES-
TABLISHMENT.

needs, sales presentations should include product demonstrations, slide shows, or documentation to highlight product or service benefits and prove your success with other customers. Whenever possible, have them sample your products and services in person as Trotter does when he invites vendors, banquet planners, and hotel concierges to visit the restaurant and taste his "product." He's confident his culinary wares will speak for themselves and require no comparisons. As such, the chef has strictly instructed his sales staff never to attack competitors—an example well worth following.

Because you pay salespeople to ultimately sell products or services, you need to train them to close the sale. Sometimes the sale is there for the asking. In less clear-cut situations, when buyers raise objections about quality, price, terms, selection, or delivery, salespeople need to provide convincing arguments regarding your product's benefits and your company's superior service and to negotiate terms. Particularly if your company sells very expensive or technical products or intangible services, it might take several attempts to close a sale. After a few phone calls or visits to the same person, it's kosher to ask buyers what's preventing them from making a purchase. When they can't reach a decision, ask buyers if they need additional information or data about your products or financing arrangements to make a decision, if they need company references, and finally if they wish to test the product or service. After the last contact, sales staff should continue calling on a weekly basis or as often as the prospect recommends unless they are given a final "no."

When a sale is made, the salesperson's job is far from complete. A business can lose its customers if it doesn't provide ongoing customer service after the sale is made. As a matter of fact, technical salespeople often are expected to train the purchaser in how to use the company's products. Generally speaking, salespeople need to continuously follow up with their clients to make sure they are satisfied with service, product quality, your company's policies, and response time. When problems are uncovered, it's the sales staff's responsibility to notify the appropriate managers in your company to make sure customer needs are met.

excellence

IN PUBLIC SERVICE

46 When You're Not Managing, Motivating, and Marketing,

Champion Causes

Corporate philanthropy, in essence an American invention, is making a resurgence on the cusp of the twenty-first century, simultaneously benefiting the society at large and strengthening the position of companies with the vision to support good causes.

After working hard to become one of the best enterprises in your community and industry, your competitors, industry observers, trade associations, analysts, and the media will undoubtedly start to take notice. The time will have come for you to use your media influence and high standing in the industry to champion good causes—in your field of work, your community, the world beyond.

Sometimes the efforts you make will go toward a campaign that is long-term and more abstract. Other times, endeavors will take on a very personal meaning. In 1997, one of Charlie Trotter's most influential and visionary colleagues, chef Patrick Clark, died at the age of forty-two while awaiting a heart transplant, leaving five young children. Clark, who was trained in the French tradition, had achieved celebrity status and served as a role model to African Americans passionate about the culinary arts. Winner of the 1995 James Beard Award for Best Mid-Atlantic Chef, Clark was lauded by the food press nationwide and credited with elevating the food at New York's Tavern on the Green to legendary status. To remember the culinary pioneer, Charlie Trotter and notable colleagues, including Thomas Keller, Jacques Pépin, Alice Waters, and Mark Miller, collaborated to memorialize Clark in the way they best knew how—through food. Together, this stellar group gathered recipes

Clark had inspired for a cookbook entitled *Cooking with Patrick Clark: A Tribute to the Man and His Cuisine,* with all royalties being donated to an education fund for Clark's children.

Improving Your Industry

Besides being an entrepreneur and businessperson, Trotter also is a trained chef working hard to improve the standing of the culinary profession. Truth be told, some chefs are great cooks but are terribly unorganized and fiscally irresponsible. That's why for years Trotter has advocated that all chefs pay attention to all aspects of the business. According to Bill Rice of the *Chicago Tribune,* "Trotter is very much part of a generation of Americans who have professionalized 'restauranting.'"

How do you jump into action if you decide you want to be part of major improvements in your industry? Before you get started, take a look at your profession and determine how it could be changed or improved. Ask yourself: Are there fundamental problems with the way my peers are trained or schooled? What would I recommend? Are my peers adequately rewarded for their efforts? What skills do my peers need to hone? From what other professions could we learn? Are industry associations and educational institutions in touch with the needs of my profession? What could they do to help? Who are the best role models and how could we together form an educational initiative? Do industry trade and business magazines adequately address our industry's issues? What could I do to influence them? Are there ethics problems in my profession? What could be done to resolve them?

Not only should you change or improve your particular industry, but also you should work to improve public perception of your profession and industry. Some professions aren't well respected; others aren't well trusted or appreciated. Clearly, attorneys, media folk, and used car salesmen have their work cut out for them. While unions and trade associations often take up these causes, consider how you might help. As part of your public relations program, publicize positive stories in your industry and profession. To find good information to share with reporters, ask yourself: What negative feelings about my industry or profession exist in the public's mind? What is being done by me and my peers to change or improve? To whom should I tell this story? Do average consumers really understand our business or know what it's like to be in our shoes? What can I and my peers do to add to the public's understanding and appreciation of our work?

At world-class restaurants, a multicourse meal usually takes three-plus hours to serve, because of the number of courses, wine pairings, the complicated preparations, the attention to detail, and so on. Nonetheless, it's not uncommon for restaurant reviewers and some customers to criticize the amount of time it takes to dine. In Trotter's mind, when one dines at a restaurant like his, the meal should be the evening's main and only activity and event. In the hopes of altering the public's perception and expectations of the dining experience, Trotter has sent e-mail messages to noted food writers and has bent lots of ears. Writes Trotter: "When you go to the symphony you don't say to the conductor: 'Conduct this faster! I want you to get through this damn score faster than you are.' You sit back and you take it in."

Mr. Entrepreneur Goes to Washington

Let's face it: you and your senior managers will have access to people in high places after you create an excellent business. To be a true champion, charitable giving is important. It's also vital you use your authority and position to defend, advocate, and fight for what you believe in.

Excellence-oriented entrepreneurs are not afraid to stand up to government interference and legislation potentially damaging to their industry. They are willing and prepared to wage a fight and enlist the support of industry associations if local or national government is being unfair or intrusive. First of all, consider how environmental, tax, consumer protection, and employment legislative bills will affect your business and industry. When you disagree with a bill or law, develop a sound, substantiated argument against its adoption. Then call your industry trade association and, ideally with their help, pitch the story to the media. You won't be alone for long: as soon as industry leaders take action, most secondary industry players quickly follow.

The Larger Picture

Charlie Trotter may be obsessed with what goes on within the four walls of his Chicago restaurant, but no one ever called him myopic. "Trotter is emphatically concerned about the world outside his restaurant's doors," writes Mariclare Barret Obis of the *Vegetarian Times*. "He cares deeply about the Earth and its creatures. He abhors factory farming and uses none of its products. The fish he serves is line-caught. His commitment to organic farming extends to seeking out organic olive and other oils. 'This is a way of life,' he [Trotter] says. 'Everything has to carry over. Like 'the loop' the eco-people talk about, it's about having a relationship with the product that comes out of the land, and the land itself. It's about how we care for waste and scrap, and having a full recycling program. It takes excessive focus."

Trotter's concern for the environment doesn't translate to pie-in-the-sky prattle, however. Good Midwesterner that he is, his convictions take the form of concrete practice. At the restaurant, Trotter works with a network of

TROTTER'S CONCERN FOR THE ENVIRONMENT DOESN'T TRANSLATE TO PIE-IN-THE-SKY PRATTLE, HOWEVER. GOOD MIDWESTERNER THAT HE IS, HIS CONVICTIONS TAKE THE FORM OF CONCRETE PRACTICE.

approximately fifty different farmers, growers, foragers, and other less conventional purveyors of fine ingredients. Says the chef: "I get amazing tiny lettuces and haricots verts from a small garden at Cabrini Green, a Chicago housing project, which is tended by teenagers and grade-school kids."

When your business is successful and well known, you'll be asked to donate time and money to charitable organizations and educational institutions. You'll need to determine what percentage of your time and resources will be spent on these commitments. Outpourings of the heart are lovely, but you'll need to be fiscally and emotionally responsible to be able to give on a consistent basis and make a real difference to the organizations or causes you choose to champion.

To find your philanthropic standing in a responsible way, you may want to choose three causes that mean the most to you—and that have a good track record in terms of efficacy, sustainability, and fiscal responsibility. When evaluating to whom you'll give money, it's essential to find out what percentage of donated funds raised actually ends up in the hands of those who need it most. A number of established groups, the Catholic Charities and United Jewish Fund, for example, are ranked the best-managed and most volunteer-based charitable organizations year after year. Others spend as much as 30 percent of the money you donate on administrative costs. To evaluate newer organizations, visit them personally or request that they send you a list of references. Then call those whom you consider reputable for an overview of the group you plan to sponsor.

Some individuals contribute their time and expertise in addition to or rather than money. Chefs are regularly asked to cook at gala events in order to raise funds for cancer research or to feed the needy. Charlie Trotter is a big believer in giving back to the community. He cooks for numerous charity events, and he also donates dinners cooked both at the restaurant and at the homes of auction winners. But Trotter's largest charitable contribution comes in the form of the restaurant's "Guest Chef for a Day" program. This certificate, available only through charities, allows the recipient to work on-site in Trotter's kitchen for a day, learning how gourmet masterworks are created. Trotter gives away twenty of these prizes each month to be sold at charity auctions. Valued at $400 each, patrons often bid as much as $3,200 to be part of the Trotter's production.

Naturally, you want to donate your time to organizations doing the most to serve their constituents. Some well-known causes include literacy, hunger, drug and alcohol rehabilitation, and physical disability. Not only will you feel better and bigger by virtue of your generosity, but the public and media will take notice, too.

INDEX